S0-BIU-223

Cookin' the Old-Time Southern Way with Venezuela

To
Lina
From
Venezuela

Biography

Venezuela Richardson spent her early years with her grandparents on a farm in Thomasville, Georgia. She was educated in a one-room schoolhouse that also served as a church. She, her brother, and the neighborhood children walked a mile each way. Lunch was corn bread carried in brown bags, and clabber milk in a tin pail. When she was thirteen, she joined her parents who were already living in New York City. As a young girl in Georgia, and at a time when food preparation was hard work, she loved preparing and cooking complete meals. Before being combined in the speckled cooking pot, vegetables had to be picked or dug up from the garden, washed, shucked, snapped or peeled. Berries and nuts were collected from bushes and trees. Cows had to be milked. Their milk was used for home-churned butter and homemade ice cream. Chickens were raised for meat and eggs. Pork was cured and stored in smokehouses. Venezuela's face lights up with a smile when she reflects back upon those days. Reflections on her childhood experiences have been included in this cookbook to help you sample the flavor of the times and people who laid the foundation for her life and professional career. As you journey back with her, experience the richness of her life and of her old-time southern recipes.

Later in life, Venezuela met, worked with, and formed lifelong friendships with many well known people. Among them were home economists Gertrude Lind and Elsa Harrington. Gertrude was so impressed with Venezuela's cooking ability that she sponsored her formal education in nutrition and culinary arts at Pratt University in New York City. Venezuela assisted Elsa in preparing salads for the Perry Como Show. She delivered the famous Pillsbury cake to Arthur Godfrey at his radio studio, and sliced it while he was on the air. She supervised the test kitchen for the advertising company of Manning, Selvege & Lee.

Lee Jordan, an announcer at WCBS, loved Venezuela's food so much that he had business cards printed for her which he gave to his friends. This proved instrumental in helping Venezuela kick off her own successful catering business in 1975, called "Cooking With Venezuela". She catered parties for numerous celebrities including Lee Jordan; actress Florence Henderson, actor Cary Grant, the Honorable John V. Lindsay, former Mayor of New York City, the McGuire Sisters, radio and television personality Arthur Godfrey, and United Nations newscaster Pauline Frederick, to name just a few.

Cookin' the Old-Time Southern Way with Venezuela

by

Venezuela Richardson

Designed by Brian Studios Designs
Illustrated by Jason Moorer

Mena Publishing
487 East Main Street, #140
Mt. Kisco, New York 10549

To David, My Beloved.

We lived happily together for forty-eight years, until his passing. During that time he supported my business endeavors with his devotion, friendship and undying love. He loved to eat my old-time southern cooking. He was always my best customer.

Design by *Brian Studios Designs*
487 E. Main St., #140, Mt.Kisco, NY 10549
ISBN # 0-9727354-0-2
First Edition 2004
Library of Congress # 2002116890

Dedicated to my grandmother Callie,
who showed how simple foods,
prepared and cooked on a wood stove,
could taste so good.

A very special thanks to . . .
Cathy Culp for encouraging me to write this book at this moment in my life.

Also special thanks to . . .
Stephany Raffio for your creativity and sticking it out through the long haul.
Thanks also to all my valued friends and family who took the time to give
their opinions of this work at various stages of its development.

Table of Contents

Grandmother's Kitchen

My grandmother had an assortment of speckled pots, seasoned iron skillets, and bowls. She had basic tools such as an eggbeater, good sharp knives, cookie sheets, pie and bread pans, rolling pin, cutting board, colander, sifter, and measuring cups. She used common drinking glasses for cutting biscuits and rolls, and forks for crimping pies. She would talk to guests and family members while cooking. My grandmother's kitchen always smelled good.

Using My Recipes

All of my recipes were tested as written. For the same results as I have achieved, follow my recipes exactly. Many of these I learned from my grandmother as I watched and helped her cook. Some are my own creations, but they are in the same style as my grandmother's.

Before starting preparations, read the entire recipe, including the ingredients. Then make sure you have all ingredients, tools and equipment at hand.

Cooking times and temperatures are very important for the success of any recipe. Use a timer if available. Check oven temperature for accuracy using a second gauge placed inside the oven.

Changing ingredients will affect the outcome of the recipes. I am aware of changes in modern cooking. These recipes, however, are from a period whose style of cooking is fast disappearing. Hence, the term "Old-Time" southern cooking. Therefore, I have not altered any of the recipes, but have put them in as they were originally prepared. If you want to alter a recipe, try preparing it at least one time the way it was cooked during that period, to experience the original texture, taste and aroma.

When everything is ready, begin and ***have fun!***

Biscuits, Breads, Muffins and Rolls

I would stand close to my grandmother holding onto her apron as she cooked. She was able to measure ingredients by eye, taking a pinch or two of salt, or a handful or so of flour or cornmeal, mixing these with other ingredients to make biscuits and rolls. The aroma of freshly baked breads filled her house. There were times when Grandmother's sideboard would be covered with fresh biscuits, rolls, muffins and delicious home-made jams and jellies.

Apple Pecan Bread

- *1 cup sugar*
- *1/2 cup lard*
- *2 eggs (lightly beaten)*
- *1 cup peeled, grated tart green apples*
- *2 cups all-purpose flour*
- *1/2 teaspoon salt*
- *1 teaspoon baking soda*
- *1 cup buttermilk*
- *1/2 teaspoon vanilla*
- *1 cup coarsely-chopped pecans*
- *3 tablespoons sugar*
- *1 teaspoon ground cinnamon*

Makes 1 loaf.

Preheat oven to 350° F. Generously grease a 9x5x3-inch loaf pan with butter. In a large bowl, cream 1 cup sugar and lard with a wooden spoon. Stir eggs and apples into creamed mixture. In a sifter, combine flour, salt, and baking soda. Sift into a medium-size bowl. Gradually add dry ingredients 1/3 at a time to creamed mixture, mixing after each addition. *Do not overmix.* Stir in buttermilk and vanilla. Lightly coat nuts with flour and fold into batter. Pour batter into pan. Mix sugar and cinnamon in a cup. Sprinkle over batter. Bake 1 hour, *or* until a knife inserted into center comes out clean. Remove from oven and let stand 10 minutes. Remove from pan and let cool on rack. Serve hot or cold.

Your Notes:

Apricot Nut Bread

- *3/4 cup finely-chopped dried apricots*
- *3/4 cup boiling water*
- *1 tablespoon butter*
- *1/2 cup sugar*
- *1/2 teaspoon salt*
- *1 egg (lightly beaten)*
- *1/2 teaspoon vanilla*
- *1/2 cup whole-wheat flour*
- *3/4 cup all-purpose flour*
- *1/2 teaspoon baking soda*
- *1 teaspoon baking powder*
- *1/2 cup chopped walnuts*

Makes 1 loaf.

Preheat oven to 350° F. Generously grease a 9x5x3-inch loaf pan with butter. In a large bowl, combine apricots, water, butter, sugar, and salt. Mix and set aside to cool. Stir in egg and vanilla. In a sifter, combine whole-wheat flour, all-purpose flour, baking soda, and baking powder. Sift into a large bowl. Add about 1/2 of apricot mixture and stir until smooth. Add remaining apricot mixture and mix to a smooth batter. Lightly coat nuts with flour. Fold into batter. Pour batter into loaf pan. Bake 50 minutes, *or* until a toothpick inserted into center comes out clean. Remove from oven and let stand 10 minutes. Then remove from pan and let cool on rack. Serve hot or cold.

Your Notes:

Banana Walnut Bread

2 cups all-purpose flour
1 1/2 teaspoons baking powder
1 teaspoon baking soda
1/2 teaspoon salt
1/2 cup butter
1 cup sugar
2 eggs
3 ripe medium-size bananas (mashed)
1/2 cup finely-chopped walnuts

Makes 1 loaf.

Preheat oven to 350º F. Generously grease a 9x5x3-inch loaf pan with butter. In a sifter, combine flour, baking powder, baking soda, and salt. Sift into a large bowl. In another bowl, cream butter with a wooden spoon. Gradually add sugar to butter, beating continuously until light and fluffy. To creamed mixture add eggs one at a time, beating after each is added. Add bananas to creamed mixture. Stir to blend. Then add dry ingredients 1/3 at a time, mixing after each addition. *Do not overmix.* Lightly coat nuts with flour. Then fold into batter. Pour batter into pan. Bake 50 to 60 minutes, *or* until a knife inserted into center comes out clean. Remove from oven and let stand for 10 minutes. Then remove from pan and let cool on a rack. Serve hot or cold.

Your Notes:

Biscuits

2	*cups all-purpose flour*	*1*	*teaspoon salt*
1/2	*teaspoon baking soda*	*1/2*	*cup lard*
3	*teaspoons baking powder*	*1*	*cup milk*
1	*tablespoon sugar*		

Makes 18.

Preheat oven to 350º F. In a sifter, combine flour, baking soda, baking powder, sugar, and salt. Sift into a large bowl. Stir until blended. Cut in lard with a pastry cutter, *or* fork, until mixture resembles coarse crumbs. Stir in milk with a fork until well blended, forming a dough. Then gently form into a ball. Place on lightly floured surface. Knead gently with fingertips 10 to 15 times. Lightly dust rolling pin with flour and roll out dough to 1/2 -inch thickness. Cut with a floured biscuit cutter, *or* a floured glass rim. Place biscuits on cookie sheet 1 inch apart. Bake 15 to 20 minutes, *or* until golden brown. Serve hot. *Although it looks great, serving hot biscuits that are wrapped in a towel will prevent steam from escaping and cause the crust to be too soft.*

Rich Biscuits: Instead of 1 cup milk, use 3/4 cup light cream. Follow directions above.

Your Notes:

Buttermilk Biscuits

2 cups all-purpose flour
1/2 teaspoon baking soda
3 teaspoons baking powder
1 tablespoon sugar
1 teaspoon salt
1/2 cup lard
1 cup buttermilk

Makes 18.

Preheat oven to 350° F. In a sifter, combine flour, baking soda, baking powder, sugar, and salt. Sift into a large bowl. Mix well. Cut in lard with a pastry cutter, *or* fork, until mixture resembles coarse crumbs. Stir in buttermilk with a fork until well blended, forming a dough. Then gently form into a ball. Place on lightly floured surface. Knead gently with fingertips 10 to 15 times. Lightly dust rolling pin with flour and roll out dough to 1/2-inch thickness. Cut with a floured biscuit cutter, *or* a floured glass rim. Place biscuits 1 inch apart on cookie sheet. Bake 15 to 20 minutes, *or* until golden brown. Serve while hot. *Although it looks great, serving hot biscuits that are wrapped in a towel will prevent steam from escaping and cause the crust to be too soft.*

Cheesy Buttermilk Biscuits: Add 1 cup grated mild cheddar cheese to dough before forming into a ball. Follow directions above.

Rich Buttermilk Biscuits: Instead of 1 cup buttermilk, use 1/4 cup buttermilk and 3/4 cup light cream. Follow directions for buttermilk biscuits.

Your Notes:

Carrot Nut Bread

1 1/2 cups all-purpose flour
1 cup sugar
1 teaspoon baking soda
1/2 teaspoon salt
1 teaspoon ground cinnamon
1/2 cup cooking oil
1/2 cup buttermilk
1 teaspoon vanilla
2 eggs (lightly beaten)
1 cup finely-grated carrots
1/2 cup finely-chopped walnuts

Makes 1 loaf.

Preheat oven to 350° F. Generously grease a 9x5x3-inch loaf pan with butter. In a sifter, combine flour, sugar, baking soda, salt, and cinnamon. Sift into a large bowl. In another bowl, combine oil, buttermilk, vanilla, and eggs. Beat until thoroughly blended. Stir in carrots. Then add dry ingredients 1/3 at a time, mixing after each addition. *Do not overmix.* Lightly coat nuts with flour. Fold into batter. Pour batter into pan. Bake 1 hour, *or* until a toothpick inserted into center comes out clean. Remove from oven. Let stand for 10 minutes. Then remove from pan and let cool on a rack. Serve hot or cold.

Your Notes:

Corn Bread

- 4 *tablespoons butter*
- 2 *cups white cornmeal*
- 1/2 *cup all-purpose flour*
- 1/2 *teaspoon baking soda*
- 1/2 *teaspoon salt*
- 1 1/2 *cups buttermilk*
- 2 *eggs*

Serves 6 to 8.

Preheat oven to 350º F. Put butter in a 10-inch iron skillet, *or* a 9x13x2-inch baking pan. Place in oven to melt butter. In a large bowl, combine cornmeal, flour, baking soda, salt, buttermilk, and eggs. Mix well to make batter. Then remove skillet from oven and pour melted butter into batter. Stir well to blend. Pour batter into hot skillet and place in oven. Bake 45 minutes, *or* until a toothpick inserted into the middle comes out clean. Serve hot with plenty of churned butter.

In different parts of the country, corn bread is made with yellow cornmeal and flour; but, most Southerners make corn bread with only white cornmeal. They use a buttered skillet sizzling hot. This method starts baking the batter immediately, making a crisp brown crust.

Your Notes:

Cracklin Bread

- *2 cups white cornmeal*
- *1 teaspoon baking powder*
- *1/2 teaspoon salt*
- *1/2 cup all-purpose flour*
- *1 1/3 cups milk (warmed)*
- *3/4 cup crumbled cracklins*
- *6 tablespoons melted butter*

Serves 6 to 8.

Preheat oven to 350° F. Grease a 9x13x2-inch baking pan with butter. In a sifter, combine cornmeal, baking powder, salt, and flour. Sift into a large bowl. Pour in milk and blend well. Add cracklins and butter. Mix thoroughly. Pour batter into baking pan. Bake 45 minutes. Serve hot with lots of churned butter.

Cracklin is the crisp skin of a roasted pig. It was cut into small pieces and stored in the smokehouse.

Your Notes:

Crusty Corn Sticks

- *1 cup all-purpose flour*
- *3 tablespoons sugar*
- *4 teaspoons baking powder*
- *3/4 teaspoon salt*
- *1/8 teaspoon cayenne pepper*
- *1 cup white cornmeal*
- *2 eggs*
- *1 cup milk*
- *1/4 cup melted lard*

Makes 18.

Preheat oven to 400° F. Generously butter a corn stick pan. In a medium-size bowl, combine flour, sugar, baking powder, salt, cayenne pepper, and cornmeal. Mix thoroughly. Add eggs, milk, and lard. Beat mixture for approximately 1 minute with a wooden spoon. Spoon into corn stick pan, filling each section 3/4 full. Bake approximately 20 minutes, *or* until golden brown. Serve with lots of churned butter.

My grandmother made her own butter. She would milk the cows, then put the milk into tin tubs which she then placed on shelves. After several hours, the cream would rise to the top. Then it was skimmed off and poured into the churn. It would be churned for 1 to 2 hours until it became butter.

Your Notes:

Hoe Cakes

1 1/2 cups white cornmeal
1 1/2 teaspoons salt
1/2 teaspoon pepper
1 1/2 cups milk (warmed)
2 teaspoons lard for each cake (Butter should not be substituted in this recipe because it burns easily.)

Makes 12 to 16.

In a medium-size bowl, combine cornmeal, salt, and pepper. Pour in milk and blend well. Let mixture stand for approximately 1 hour. Heat lard, 8 teaspoons for every 4 hoe cakes, in an iron skillet until hot. Use 2 rounded tablespoons of cornmeal mixture to make each hoe cake. Put hoe cakes into skillet, 4 at a time. *Too many at one time will reduce the lard's temperature.* Use a tablespoon to flatten each to 1/2-inch thickness. Brown on both sides. Put cooked hoe cakes on brown paper to absorb excess fat. Serve hot.

Hoe cakes were cooked on a well-cleaned garden hoe over an open fire. A hoe was a common field tool, having a flat angled blade attached to a long wooden handle.

Your Notes:

Hot Pepper Corn Bread

1 cup white cornmeal
3/4 teaspoon baking soda
1/2 teaspoon salt
1/4 cup melted lard
2 eggs (lightly beaten)
1/4 cup grated onion
1 cup buttermilk
1 (8oz.) can cream style corn
2 small green chili peppers (seeded, chopped)
1 cup grated mild cheddar cheese

Serves 6 to 8.

Preheat oven to 350° F. Generously grease a 10-inch iron skillet, *or* a 9x13x2-inch baking pan with butter. In a medium-size bowl, combine cornmeal, baking soda, and salt. Add lard, eggs, onion, buttermilk, corn, and peppers. Stir well. Pour half the batter into skillet. Sprinkle 1/2 cup cheese over batter. Pour remaining batter over cheese. Then sprinkle remaining cheese over batter. Bake about 25 minutes, *or* until a knife inserted into center comes out clean. Serve with chicken.

Your Notes:

Hush Puppies

- 2 *cups white cornmeal*
- 3 *teaspoons baking powder*
- 1 *teaspoon baking soda*
- 1 *teaspoon salt*
- 2 *tablespoons all-purpose flour*
- 1/4 *teaspoon cayenne pepper*
- 1 *egg*
- 1/3 *cup finely-chopped onion*
- 2 *cups buttermilk*
- 3/4 *cup lard*

Makes 24.

Combine cornmeal, baking powder, baking soda, salt, flour, and cayenne pepper in a large bowl. Stir until completely mixed. In another bowl, combine egg, onion, and buttermilk. Stir to blend. Add buttermilk mixture to dry ingredients. Mix with a wooden spoon until it reaches a soft dough consistency. Heat lard in a large iron skillet. Cut rounded teaspoonfuls from dough. Drop into hot lard, not more than 4 at a time. *Too many at one time will make the temperature of the lard too low.* Fry until golden brown. Drain on brown paper to remove excess fat. Great alone, or with fried fish.

Flour came in cotton sacks which sometimes had designs on them. Grandmother would save them to make curtains for the kitchen windows. She and a few other women would sit around sewing quilts from the flour sacks and other materials on hand.

Your Notes:

Icebox Biscuit Mix

- *6 cups all-purpose flour*
- *3 teaspoons baking powder*
- *2 tablespoons sugar*
- *2 cups lard*
- *2/3 cup milk for each 2 cups of mixture*

Makes 48 biscuits.

Preheat oven to 350º F. In a sifter, combine flour, baking powder, and sugar. Sift into a large bowl. Cut in lard with a fork until mixture resembles coarse crumbs. Store in a covered container in icebox. *Chilled mixture will keep for several days.*

When ready to make biscuits: For each 12 biscuits, put 2 cups of mixture in a large bowl. Add 2/3 cup milk and stir with a fork until well blended. Place mixture on lightly floured surface and roll out to 1/4 -inch thickness. Cut out biscuits using a lightly floured biscuit cutter, *or* a floured glass. Place 1/4 inch apart on cookie sheet. Bake 15 to 20 minutes, *or* until golden brown. Serve with churned butter or homemade jelly.

In my grandparents' day, most homes had an icebox. It contained two sides -- one stored the ice block, the other stored the food. The ice man came often. He carried the ice in on his shoulder and placed it in the storage side. Both sides were cold within a few hours.

Your Notes:

Icebox Rolls

2 packages active dry yeast
1/2 cup warm water
1 cup milk
3/4 cup lard
1/3 cup sugar
2 teaspoons salt
1 cup hot mashed potatoes
2 eggs (lightly beaten)
6 to 8 cups sifted all-purpose flour

Makes 36 rolls.

Day One: Dissolve yeast in warm water. Set aside. Pour milk into a large saucepot. Heat until very hot. *Do not boil.* Remove from stove and add lard, sugar, salt, and mashed potatoes. Stir mixture until lard melts. Then pour into a large bowl and set aside. When mixture is cool, add eggs and yeast. Gradually add flour while beating. *When dough is stiff you have used enough flour.* Place dough on lightly floured surface. Use remaining flour, if necessary, and knead approximately 10 minutes, *or* until dough is smooth. Grease a large bowl with lard. Shape dough into a ball and roll gently in bowl until lightly coated. Cover bowl tightly. Place in icebox overnight. *For best flavor use icebox dough within 36 to 48 hours.*

Day Two: Remove dough from icebox. Cut into 3 equal portions. *Each portion will make 12 rolls. Any portion not being used should immediately be covered tightly and returned to icebox.* Allow dough to reach room temperature before shaping rolls. Generously grease a muffin pan with lard. Divide each portion of dough into 36 pieces about 1 inch in size. Using the palms of your hands, roll pieces into balls. Place 3 balls in bottom of each muffin cup. Cover with a towel and put in a warm place away from drafts. Let dough rise until doubled in size, about 45 minutes. After 30 minutes, preheat oven to 325° F. Bake about 30 minutes, *or* until golden brown. Remove pan from oven. Use a fork to slightly lift and tilt each roll. (This stops the cooking process and permits the heat to escape.) Rolls are best served hot straight from the pan.

Mother's Buttermilk Rolls

- *1/4 cup warm water*
- *1 envelope active dry yeast*
- *2 cups buttermilk*
- *5 cups all-purpose flour*
- *1 teaspoon baking powder*
- *1 teaspoon baking soda*
- *1 teaspoon salt*
- *2 tablespoons sugar*
- *4 tablespoons lard*

Makes 36 large rolls or 48 small rolls.

Put warm water in a measuring cup. Add yeast and stir until dissolved. Add 3/4 cup buttermilk to yeast and set aside. In a medium-size bowl, combine flour, baking powder, baking soda, and salt. In another bowl, using a wooden spoon, cream sugar and lard until smooth and creamy. Alternate adding flour mixture, yeast mixture and remaining buttermilk. Mix well after each addition. Dough will be soft. Lightly grease another bowl with lard. Gently shape dough into a ball and place in greased bowl. Roll around until lightly coated. *Do not overhandle.* Cover and put into icebox until ready to use. *Icebox dough will keep for several days.*

When ready to bake: Remove dough from icebox. Cut dough into 3 equal portions for large rolls, *or* 4 equal portions for small rolls. For each 12 rolls, use 1 portion of dough. Cover unused portions and put back in icebox for later use. Divide each portion into 12 pieces and form into balls. Place on a cookie sheet about 1/2 inch apart. Cover with a towel, and put in a warm place away from drafts. Let rise until doubled in size, approximately 2 hours. Heat oven to 375º F. Bake 20 minutes, *or* until golden brown. Serve hot anytime with lots of churned butter or your favorite homemade preserves.

Grandmother put dough that she wanted to rise
in the warmer above the wood burning stove.

Grandmother's Wood-Burning Stove

Grandmother could put her hand in the oven of her wood-burning stove and know when the temperature was just right for cooking. She seldom burned or overcooked anything.

No-Knead White Bread

2 1/2 cups warm water
2 packages dry active yeast
4 tablespoons lard (melted)
4 teaspoons salt
4 tablespoons sugar
6 cups sifted all-purpose flour
3 tablespoons butter (melted)

Makes 2 loaves.

Generously grease two 9x5x3-inch loaf pans with lard. Put water in a large bowl. Add yeast and stir until dissolved. Add lard, salt, and sugar, and stir to blend. While stirring, slowly add 3 cups flour. Beat mixture with a wooden spoon, scraping sides and bottom of bowl, until well blended. Slowly add remaining flour while continuing to beat. Beat until batter is smooth. Cover bowl with a towel. Put in a warm place away from drafts. Let rise until doubled in size, about 30 minutes. When dough has risen, stir down by beating 30 to 40 strokes. Divide dough in half and spread evenly in loaf pans. Cover pans and put in a warm place away from drafts. Let rise to 1/4 inch from top of pans. *Allow about 40 minutes.* Heat oven to 350° F. Bake 45 to 50 minutes. *When the bread rises fully, the top should be rounded, golden brown and crisp.* Remove from oven and immediately turn loaves onto cake racks to cool. Leave uncovered and away from drafts. Brush top of loaves with butter.

Your Notes:

Popovers

1 cup sifted all-purpose flour
1/4 teaspoon salt
2 eggs
1 cup milk
1 tablespoon melted butter

Makes 6 to 8 large popovers.

Preheat oven to 425° F. Generously grease 6 to 8 custard cups, *or* a muffin pan with butter. For easy handling, place cups on a cookie sheet. Place in oven to heat. Into a medium-size bowl, sift flour and salt. In another bowl, beat eggs with a fork until light and fluffy. Add milk and melted butter. Gradually add dry ingredients, beating until mixture is smooth. Remove custard cups from oven. Pour batter into cups to 1/3 full. Return to hot oven. Bake 30 minutes. *To prevent popovers from collapsing and becoming soggy, do not open oven door during first 30 minutes of cooking.* Then reduce heat to 350° F and bake 15 minutes longer. A few minutes before removing popovers from oven, prick each one to allow steam to escape.

Your Notes:

Sour Cream Corn Bread

- *1/2 cup butter*
- *1 cup cream style corn*
- *1 cup sour cream*
- *1/2 cup all-purpose flour*
- *2 teaspoons baking powder*
- *1/4 teaspoon baking soda*
- *1 cup white cornmeal*
- *2 eggs (lightly beaten)*
- *1/4 cup grated onion*

Serves 4 to 6.

Preheat oven to 350º F. Put butter in a 8-inch iron skillet. Place in oven to melt butter. In a large bowl, combine corn, sour cream, flour, baking powder, baking soda, cornmeal, eggs, and onion. Mix well. Pour butter into batter. Stir to blend. Then pour batter into the hot skillet. Bake 35 to 40 minutes. Serve hot.

Many quick breads were cooked in iron skillets in the oven or on top of the stove.

Your Notes:

Spicy-Hot Corn Muffins

3 cups white cornmeal
2 1/2 cups milk
3 eggs (lightly beaten)
1/2 cup melted lard
2 tablespoons sugar
1/2 cup chopped green chili peppers
1/2 cup grated mild cheddar cheese
1/4 pound fried crisp and crumbled bacon
1/4 cup chopped pimientos
1 clove crushed garlic
1 cup cream style corn
1 large grated onion
1/4 teaspoon cayenne pepper

Makes 12.

Preheat oven to 400º F. Generously grease a muffin pan with lard. In a large bowl, combine cornmeal, milk, and eggs to make batter. Mix well. Pour in lard and add sugar, chili peppers, cheese, bacon, pimientos, garlic, corn, onion, and cayenne pepper. Stir until all ingredients are mixed. *Do not overmix*. Fill muffin cups 2/3 full. Bake 35 to 40 minutes. Excellent with barbecued ribs.

Your Notes:

Spoon Bread

- *2 cups white cornmeal*
- *2 cups boiling water*
- *1 1/4 cups milk*
- *1/4 cup sugar*
- *1 teaspoon salt*
- *3 heaping tablespoons lard (melted)*
- *3 eggs (separated)*

Serves 6 to 8.

Separate eggs while they are cold. Crack each egg and separate whites into one small bowl and yolks into a second bowl.

Preheat oven to 350º F. Generously grease a large iron skillet with lard. Place cornmeal in a large bowl. Slowly stir in water until cornmeal is dissolved and there are no lumps. Add milk, sugar, salt, and lard. Beat well until blended. Beat egg yolks until creamy and add to mixture. Mix well. Beat egg whites until stiff peaks form. Then gently fold into mixture. Pour batter into skillet. Bake 30 to 35 minutes, *or* until a knife inserted into center comes out clean. Spoon hot onto plates.

Your Notes:

Soups, Stews, Gumbos and Jambalayas

Grandmother would go into her garden and get snap beans, fresh greens, green black-eyed peas, and tomatoes. She would pick a few ears of corn from the field, dig up about five white potatoes, and cut a head of cabbage, all to go into the soup. My brother and I had to remove the stems from the beans and break them in half. We would shell the black-eyed peas and shuck the corn. Then we could go out to play.

Beef Stew

- *1/3 cup lard*
- *1/3 cup flour*
- *4 pounds beef (cut into 1 1/2-inch cubes)*
- *4 fresh tomatoes (cubed)*
- *6 medium potatoes (cubed)*
- *2 large onions (diced)*
- *4 large carrots (cut into 1/4-inch rounds)*
- *1 cup fresh green peas*
- *1 cup water*

Serves 6 to 8.

Melt lard in a large deep skillet over medium-high heat. Place flour on a large plate and dredge beef cubes in flour. Add beef to skillet and stir until lightly brown on all sides. Cover skillet and cook over medium heat for 30 minutes, stirring often. Add tomatoes, potatoes, carrots, onions and peas. Continue cooking over low heat for 1 hour. Add water and continue cooking for 30 minutes.

Your Notes:

Black-Eyed Pea Soup with Baked Yams

- *1 pound shelled green black-eyed peas*
- *12 cups cold water*
- *2 pounds smoked neck bones*
- *1 cup chopped onion*
- *2 chicken bouillon cubes*
- *1 (8 oz.) can tomato sauce*
- *8 small yams*
- *1/3 cup lard*
- *1 bunch scallions (thinly sliced)*

Serves 8.

Sort peas in a colander. Discard any bad ones. Rinse remaining peas thoroughly under cold running water. Put peas in a large bowl and set aside. Use a vegetable brush to scrub yams thoroughly under cold running water. Pat dry with a towel. Remove and discard any stems. Wash neck bones thoroughly under cold running water. In a large pot, combine water, neck bones, onion, bouillon cubes, and tomato sauce. Bring to a boil. Lower heat and cook 1 1/2 hours. Then add peas to pot. Cook until peas are tender, about 1 hour more.

While peas are cooking: Preheat oven to 325º F. Grease yams well with lard and place on a large cookie sheet. Bake until tender, about 45 minutes. Remove from oven, let cool, and peel. Place a yam in each soup bowl and cover with black-eyed pea soup. Top with scallions. Serve hot with bread. *(See my recipes.)*

Your Notes:

Carrot Barley Soup

4 tablespoons butter
1 cup coarsely-chopped onion
1 meaty turkey frame (broken into pieces)
8 cups chicken broth
1 cup pearl barley
2 teaspoons salt
1/2 teaspoon pepper
4 carrots
2 parsnips
2 tablespoons chopped fresh parsley

Serves 6.

Melt butter in a large pot. Add onion and cook until transparent, about 5 minutes. *Do not brown.* Add turkey, chicken broth, barley, salt, and pepper. Put lid on and bring to a boil. Lower heat. Simmer 1 hour, stirring occasionally. Rinse and peel carrots and parsnips. Cut carrots into 1-inch rounds. Cut parsnips into 1/2 -inch rounds. Add carrots and parsnips to pot. Put lid back on and continue simmering 30 minutes more. Stir in parsley. Serve immediately.

Grandmother usually made this soup right after Thanksgiving. She would snap the turkey bones into pieces and place them in the speckled soup pot.

Your Notes:

Catfish Stew

- *3 pounds catfish (skinned, cleaned, boned)*
- *1 cup water*
- *1 cup diced white potatoes*
- *1 cup diced carrots*
- *2 teaspoons salt*
- *1 teaspoon pepper*
- *1/4 cup bacon drippings*
- *1 cup sliced onion*
- *2 cups milk*
- *1/2 teaspoon rosemary*
- *1/4 teaspoon thyme*
- *2 tablespoons all-purpose flour*
- *1 cup light cream*

Serves 4.

(See page 105, How to clean and fillet fresh catfish.) Cut catfish into 2-inch chunks and place in icebox. Put water, potatoes, carrots, salt and pepper in a large pot. Put lid on pot and simmer 20 minutes, *or* until carrots are tender. Heat bacon drippings in an iron skillet over low heat. Add onion and cook 5 minutes, *or* until tender. *Do not brown.* Add onions to pot. Slowly stir in milk, rosemary, and thyme. Combine flour and cream in a medium-size bowl and stir until smooth. Slowly add flour mixture to pot while stirring. Then add catfish and put lid on pot. Simmer until thick and catfish is tender when pierced with a fork, about 20 minutes longer. Serve hot with corn bread. *(See my recipes.)*

Your Notes:

Chicken Jambalaya

- *3 cups medium-size shrimp (peeled, deveined)*
- *1 ($3^1/_2$-pound) frying chicken*
- *$^3/_4$ cup all-purpose flour*
- *2 teaspoons salt*
- *1 teaspoon white pepper*
- *$^1/_4$ cup lard*
- *$^1/_4$ cup butter*
- *2 medium-size onions (thinly sliced)*
- *4 garlic cloves (coarsely chopped)*
- *1 teaspoon chili pepper (coarsely chopped)*
- *1 large green pepper (thinly sliced lengthwise)*
- *1 tablespoon sugar*
- *3 dashes hot pepper sauce*
- *2 ripe medium-size tomatoes (skinned, diced)*
- *$^1/_2$ pound ham (diced)*
- *4 teaspoons tomato paste*
- *$2^1/_2$ cups dry white wine (original recipe used $^1/_2$ cup of Grandfather's corn likker)*

Serves 6 to 8.

Using a colander, rinse shrimp under cold running water. Put in a bowl and place in icebox. Wash chicken thoroughly, pat dry and cut into serving pieces *(see page 92 for instructions)*. Combine flour, salt, and white pepper in a brown paper bag. Put chicken, a few pieces at a time, in bag and shake to coat. Set aside. Melt lard in a large iron skillet. Add chicken pieces to hot skillet. Fry until lightly brown on each side. Place on brown paper to absorb excess fat. In a large saucepot melt butter over medium heat. Add onion, garlic, chili pepper, green pepper, sugar, hot pepper sauce, and tomatoes. Cook 5 minutes, stirring frequently. Add ham, shrimp, and tomato paste to saucepot and stir. Cook 5 minutes. Add chicken and wine and stir. Cover and cook over low heat 30 minutes, *or* until chicken is tender, and all liquid is absorbed. Serve hot over rice or mashed potatoes.

Your Notes:

Chicken Oyster Gumbo

- *1 (2 1/2 to 3-pound) frying chicken*
- *2 tablespoons bacon drippings*
- *1/2 pound spicy hot sausages*
- *1 cup chopped onion*
- *2 tablespoons all-purpose flour*
- *2 tablespoons minced parsley*
- *3 cups water*
- *1 teaspoon salt*
- *1/4 teaspoon black pepper*
- *1/4 teaspoon cayenne pepper*
- *1 bay leaf*
- *1 dozen live oysters*
- *1 teaspoon filé*

Serves 6 to 8.

Wash chicken under cold running water and pat dry. Cut into serving pieces *(see page 92 for instructions)*. Heat bacon drippings in a large pot. Add chicken and lightly brown on both sides. Remove chicken from pot, place on brown paper and set aside. *Leave bacon drippings in pot.* Rinse sausages under cold running water. Cut into 1/4 -inch rounds. Brown sausage in bacon drippings. Remove sausage from pot, place on brown paper and set aside. Add onion to pot and cook until transparent. *Do not brown.* While stirring, add flour and parsley. Gradually add water while stirring constantly. Return chicken and sausage to pot. Add salt, black pepper, cayenne pepper, and bay leaf. Cover and simmer until chicken is tender, about 1 hour. Using a colander, rinse oysters under cold running water and shuck. Add oysters to pot and cook until oysters curl at edges. Remove bay leaf from pot and discard. Just before serving, sprinkle 1/8 -teaspoon filé into each serving bowl. Cover with gumbo and stir. Serve immediately.

Substituting okra for filé: Add 1 cup thinly sliced okra to pot after chicken has cooked 45 minutes.

Fisherman's Catch

- *1 1/2 pounds wheat fish*
- *2 pounds sea bass*
- *1 1/2 pounds catfish*
- *1 1/2 cups dry white wine (original recipe used 1/2 cup of Grandfather's corn likker)*
- *3 1/2 cups cold water*
- *2 garlic cloves (coarsely chopped)*
- *1/2 cup chopped shallots*
- *1 cup chopped onion*
- *1/2 teaspoon thyme*
- *1/4 teaspoon tarragon*
- *1 bay leaf*
- *5 sprigs fresh parsley (chopped)*
- *1/2 teaspoon salt*
- *1/2 teaspoon cayenne pepper*
- *8 tablespoons butter (room temperature)*
- *8 tablespoons all-purpose flour*
- *6 tablespoons bacon drippings*

Serves 6 to 8.

Rinse fish under cold running water. Clean and bone fish. Rinse again. Cut fish into 2-inch pieces. Put in a bowl, cover, and place in icebox. Pour wine and water into a large pot. Stir in garlic, shallots, onion, thyme, tarragon, bay leaf, parsley, salt, and cayenne pepper. Bring to a boil. Lower heat and simmer 1 hour. Using a wooden spoon, cream 4 tablespoons butter in a small bowl. Gradually stir flour into butter until smooth and well blended. Slowly add 1/2 cup of liquid from pot to flour mixture, stirring until smooth. Slowly stir flour mixture into pot until mixture thickens. Remove fish from icebox and pat dry. In a large iron skillet, combine bacon drippings with remaining butter and melt over medium heat. For best results, cook only a few pieces at a time. *Too many pieces at one time will make the temperature of the oil too low.* Lightly brown fish on both sides. Add fish to pot, put lid on, and simmer 20 minutes more. Remove bay leaf. Spoon soup into a large bowl. Sprinkle with parsley.

Country Store

When the men went to the country store to get flour, sugar, cornmeal and other staples, they would be given a large bag of chicken feet which they later divided between three families. The men would also clean the chicken feet which were used in making homemade soup.

Garden Vegetable Soup

- *12 chicken feet*
- *12 cups cold water*
- *1 ham bone*
- *1/2 cup butter*
- *2 teaspoons salt*
- *2 teaspoons pepper*
- *2 cups diced onion*
- *2 cups fresh corn (cut from cob)*
- *2 cups snap beans (string beans)*
- *2 cups green black-eyed peas*
- *2 cups diced fresh tomatoes*
- *2 cups chopped green cabbage*
- *4 tablespoons bacon drippings*

Serves 8 to 12.

Wash chicken feet under cold running water. Pour water into a large pot. Add ham bone, chicken feet, butter, salt, and pepper. Bring to a boil. Add onion, corn, beans, black-eyed peas, tomato, and cabbage. Bring to a second boil. Lower heat and simmer uncovered for 1 hour. Stir in bacon drippings. Cover and simmer 30 minutes longer. Delicious served hot with homemade breads or biscuits. *(See my recipes.)*

Bacon drippings were kept in a container on the back of the stove and were used for seasoning and frying.

Your Notes:

Hearty Barley Soup with Chicken Backs

12 cups cold water
4 celery stalks
8 carrots
2 large onions
2 teaspoons chopped fresh parsley
3 teaspoons salt
1 teaspoon pepper
1/4 teaspoon thyme
3/4 cup coarse barley
3 pounds chicken backs

Serves 6 to 8.

Pour water into a large pot and bring to a boil. Wash celery and carrots under cold running water. Peel carrots. Chop celery and carrots into 1/4-inch pieces. Chop onions coarsely. Add celery, onions, parsley, salt, pepper, thyme, and barley to pot. Put lid on and simmer over low heat 1 hour 30 minutes. Rinse chicken under cold running water. Add chicken and carrots to pot and put lid back on. Cook 45 minutes longer, *or* until meat falls off bones. *This soup will be very thick. You can almost eat it with a fork.*

Your Notes:

Red Snapper Stew

4 celery stalks
8 large carrots
4 tablespoons bacon drippings
4 medium-size onions (chopped)
4 medium-size green peppers (chopped)
2 garlic cloves (coarsely chopped)
2 tablespoons all-purpose flour
12 cups cold water
4 pounds red snapper (cleaned, boned)
1 teaspoon thyme
1 bay leaf
2 teaspoons salt
2 teaspoons black pepper
6 large tomatoes (chopped)
2 tablespoons chopped parsley

Serves 8 to 12.

Wash celery and carrots under cold running water. Peel carrots. Chop celery and carrots into 1/4-inch pieces. In a large pot, combine bacon drippings, onions, green peppers, garlic, carrots, and celery. Cook over medium heat until tender, about 5 minutes. Sprinkle flour into pot while stirring with a wooden spoon. Gradually add water, stirring constantly. Cut fish into bite-size pieces and add to pot. Add thyme, bay leaf, salt, black pepper, and stir. Bring to a rapid boil. Reduce heat. Simmer 1 1/2 hours. Add tomatoes and parsley. Continue simmering 30 minutes longer. Great with homemade bread or rolls. *(See my recipes.)*

Your Notes:

Seafood Gumbo

- *8 slices bacon (coarsely chopped)*
- *2 tablespoons all-purpose flour*
- *1 garlic clove (coarsely chopped)*
- *1 1/2 cups finely-chopped onion*
- *1/2 cup diced celery*
- *4 cups sliced fresh okra*
- *1 cup diced green pepper*
- *6 cups boiling water*
- *2 pounds small shrimp (shelled, deveined)*
- *2 pounds fresh crab meat*
- *1/2 pint fresh oysters*
- *2 teaspoons hot pepper sauce*
- *1 tablespoon Worcestershire sauce*
- *1/2 cup minced fresh parsley*
- *1/2 cup sliced scallions*
- *2 teaspoons salt*
- *1 teaspoon black pepper*

Serves 12.

Fry bacon in a large pot over medium heat. Reduce heat and slowly stir in flour. Cook about 5 minutes more, stirring until flour browns. Stir in garlic, onion, celery, okra, and green pepper. Continue cooking 10 minutes, stirring often. Add boiling water slowly and stir to blend. Cover, continue cooking 20 minutes. Add shrimp, crab meat, oysters, hot pepper sauce, and Worcestershire sauce. Stir well. Cover and continue cooking 5 minutes. Remove from heat. Add parsley, scallions, salt, and black pepper. Stir well. Serve hot over rice.

Your Notes:

Shrimp Jambalaya

- *1 pound pork sausages*
- *4 tablespoons lard*
- *1 cup chopped onion*
- *1 garlic clove (minced)*
- *2 green peppers (chopped)*
- *1 (16 oz.) jar whole tomatoes with juice*
- *1 teaspoon salt*
- *1/2 teaspoon red pepper*
- *1/2 teaspoon thyme*
- *2 tablespoons Worcestershire sauce*
- *2 cups shrimp (cleaned, deveined)*
- *2 tablespoons minced fresh parsley*
- *1/2 cup cold water*
- *3 cups cooked rice*

Serves 10 to 12.

Rinse sausages under cold running water. Cut into 1/2-inch pieces. Melt lard in a large deep iron skillet, *or* large pot. Fry sausage over medium heat until browned. Pour off fat, leaving about 2 tablespoons. Add onion, garlic, and green pepper to skillet. Cook 5 minutes over low heat, stirring occasionally. Put tomatoes with their juice in a bowl. Cut tomatoes into chunks. Add tomatoes with their juice, salt, red pepper, thyme, and Worcestershire sauce to skillet. Stir, cover and simmer 15 minutes. Add shrimp, parsley, water, and rice. Mix well. Cover and simmer 20 minutes longer, stirring only once.

Your Notes:

Vegetables

Grandfather, Mr. Scruggs and Mr. Thomas had large farms with lots of vegetables. They each planted tomatoes, collard greens, sweet potatoes, yams, beans, sugar cane, and a lot more. Each would also have crops that the others didn't, and when it came time, they would work together and share the harvest.

Bacon and Vegetables

- *8 slices lean bacon*
- *1 (16 oz.) jar stewed tomatoes*
- *1 (16 oz.) jar whole kernel corn (do not drain)*
- *1/4 teaspoon cayenne pepper*
- *1 teaspoon salt*
- *1 pound fresh okra*

Serves 4 to 6.

In a large iron skillet, fry bacon over medium heat until brown and crisp. Remove bacon from skillet and place on brown paper. Pour bacon drippings into a large saucepot. Add tomatoes, corn, cayenne pepper, and salt. Wash okra under cold running water and pat dry. Cut off and discard tops and bottoms of okra. Cut into 2-inch pieces. Add to pot. Cover and simmer 30 minutes. Place vegetables in a serving dish. Crumble bacon and sprinkle a teaspoon on each serving. Enjoy with hot corn bread. *(See my recipes.)*

Grandmother didn't like canning, but she would help the neighbors. They gathered at Mrs. Scruggs' house to prepare all their vegetables and fruits. It took a whole day to can each vegetable and each fruit. They each took their share home at the end of the day.

Your Notes:

Peanuts

Boiled peanuts were a real treat during peanut-picking time. Grandfather would dig them up early in the morning. Grandmother would wash and boil them. For hours we would sit on the porch eating boiled peanuts, sharing them with anyone who stopped by.

Boiled Peanuts

8 - 10 pounds fresh green peanuts (with shell)
1 cup salt

Rinse peanuts under cold running water. Place peanuts in a large pot and cover with cold water. Add salt. Bring to a rapid boil. Lower heat and simmer 4 hours uncovered. Add water when necessary to keep peanuts covered. Drain. Let cool. Serve in a bowl.

Your Notes:

Candied Yams

4 pounds medium-size yams
1 1/2 cups orange juice
2 cups firmly-packed light brown sugar
3 tablespoons fresh lemon juice
1 cup butter (melted)

Serves 12.

Preheat oven to 375° F. Generously butter a 9x13x2-inch baking pan. Wash yams well under cold running water. Cut off any stems. Place in a large pot and cover with cold water. Bring to a rapid boil. Lower heat. Cook 30 minutes, *or* until tender. Use a colander to drain yams and let cool. Peel and slice each yam into 1/4 -inch pieces. Set aside. In a small bowl, combine orange juice, brown sugar, and lemon juice. Stir well. Place a layer of yams in the pan. Pour 1/2 the brown sugar mixture over yams. Then pour 1/2 cup butter over yams. Add a second layer of the remaining yams. Then pour remaining brown sugar mixture and butter on top. Bake 45 minutes. Baste occasionally with juices in pan.

Grandmother would keep food in the warmer above the stove until she was ready to serve it.

Your Notes:

Corn Fritters

- 6 *fresh ears of corn (in husks), or*
  1 (16 oz.) can whole kernel corn (drained)
- 3 *eggs (separated)*
- 1 *cup all-purpose flour*
- 1/2 *teaspoon paprika*
- 1 *tablespoon sugar*
- 1 *teaspoon salt*
- 2 *teaspoons baking powder*
- 3/4 *cup lard*

Makes 12.

Separate eggs while they are cold. Crack each egg and separate whites into one small bowl and yolks into a second bowl.

Remove husks and silk from corn. Rinse corn quickly under cold running water. Cut off tips of ears. Cut kernels from cobs with a sharp knife. *Do not cut all the way to the cob.* Discard cobs, and set aside kernels. In a large bowl, beat egg yolks well. Add corn, flour, paprika, sugar, salt, and baking powder. Mix well. In a medium-size bowl, beat egg whites until stiff. Fold into egg yolk mixture. Melt lard in a 12-inch iron skillet over medium-high heat. Scoop rounded tablespoons from batter. Use a second spoon to push batter immediately into hot lard. Work quickly. Cook 6 at a time. *Too many at one time will make the temperature of the lard too low.* Make sure lard stays hot during cooking. Adjust heat if necessary. Fry 4 to 5 minutes, *or* until golden brown, turning once. Place on brown paper to absorb excess fat. Serve hot with corn syrup or molasses.

Your Notes:

Fried Cabbage

- *1 large cabbage*
- *1/2 pound fatback*
- *1/2 cup cold water*
- *2 teaspoons salt*
- *1 teaspoon pepper*

Serves 4 to 6.

Remove and discard outer leaves of cabbage. Also discard any discolored and damaged leaves. Cut cabbage into quarters. Then cut away and discard core. Slice cabbage thinly and set aside. Slice fatback thinly and put in a large heavy pot. Fry over medium heat until fat is rendered. Remove fatback with a slotted spoon and discard. Put cabbage in pot. Add water, salt, and pepper. Stir, put lid on and lower heat. Simmer 30 minutes. Then remove lid and stir. Continue to cook uncovered. After water has evaporated, cook 2 to 3 minutes more. Stir occasionally to prevent cabbage from sticking to bottom of pot. Cabbage will have a light brown color when done.

Your Notes:

Fried Fresh Corn

6 fresh ears of corn (in husks)
1/2 pound fatback (thinly sliced)
1 teaspoon sugar
1/2 cup light cream
1/4 teaspoon salt
1/2 teaspoon pepper
2 tablespoons all-purpose flour

Serves 4 to 6.

Remove husks and silk from corn. Rinse corn quickly under cold running water. Cut off tips of ears. Cut kernels from cobs with a sharp knife. *Do not cut all the way to the cob.* Then scrape cob downward with back of knife to remove remaining pulp and juice. Set kernels and juice aside and discard cobs. Fry fatback in a large iron skillet until fat is rendered. Remove fatback with a slotted spoon and discard. Combine corn, sugar, cream, salt, and pepper in skillet. Simmer 30 minutes. Stir often to keep corn from sticking. Sprinkle in flour slowly, stirring constantly. Continue to cook and stir 10 minutes more. Serve hot.

Your Notes:

Fried Green Tomatoes

4 1/2	*cups white cornmeal*	*8*	*large green tomatoes*
2	*teaspoons salt*	*1*	*cup lard*
1/4	*teaspoon cayenne pepper*	*2*	*eggs*

Serves 8 to 10.

In a medium-size bowl, combine cornmeal, salt, and cayenne pepper. Stir to blend. Gently rinse tomatoes under cold running water and wipe dry. Slice tomatoes into 1/4 -inch rounds and set aside. Melt lard in a large iron skillet over medium heat. Beat eggs until light and fluffy. Dip tomato slices in egg. Then coat with cornmeal mixture. Fry until golden brown on both sides, turning only once. *Watch carefully to prevent burning.* Place on a brown paper bag to absorb excess fat. Great as a breakfast side dish.

Grandmother had a small garden just outside the back door where she planted lettuce, tomatoes, peas and string beans, just to name a few. She would send me out early in the morning to pick the vegetables for that day.

Your Notes:

Fried Yams

3 large yams
2 tablespoons salt
1/2 cup butter
1/3 cup sugar
1/2 cup cold water

Serves 6 to 8.

Peel yams. Slice each yam into 3 thick slices lengthwise. Put into a large bowl. Then add salt and cover with cold water. Let soak 1 hour. Then drain. Heat butter in a large iron skillet over medium heat until hot. Fry slices lightly on both sides. Sprinkle sugar on yams. Add water. Put lid on and simmer 20 minutes. Remove lid and continue cooking until liquid looks like thick syrup, about 10 minutes longer. Makes a great side dish.

Your Notes:

Georgia Corn Pudding

4 cups fresh white corn cut from cob
6 eggs (lightly beaten)
4 tablespoons sugar
3 teaspoons salt
1 teaspoon pepper
8 tablespoons butter (melted)

Serves 8.

Preheat oven to 350º F. Generously butter a 3-quart casserole dish. In a medium-size bowl, combine corn, eggs, sugar, salt, pepper, and butter. Stir well to blend. Pour mixture into casserole dish. Set in a pan of warm water. Bake until firm, approximately 1 hour 15 minutes, *or* until a knife inserted into center comes out clean. Serve with main course. It's delicious!

Your Notes:

Grilled Fresh Corn in the Husk

6 ears fresh corn (in husks)
6 teaspoons butter

Serves 6.

Pull husks down, *but do not remove.* Pull off and discard silk. Smear butter over ears. Pull husks back up. Wet husks well under cold running water. Place on grill over glowing coals. Turn corn often to prevent burning. Grill approximately 35 to 45 minutes, *depending upon the size of the ears.* Husks will appear scorched. Remove from grill. Serve immediately.

Your Notes:

New Year's Eve

New Year's Eve was very special. Our family got all dressed up and went to midnight service. Afterwards, we enjoyed good home cooking with the neighbors. Each year this celebration would be at a different home, but pig feet, collard greens, black-eyed peas, and rice were always served. On this day Grandfather always made sure we each had a dollar in our pockets. He said the dollar was a tradition -- it meant we would have money all year. Today I still make sure I have a dollar in my purse on New Year's Eve and I always have money the year round.

Ham Hocks, Collard Greens and Cabbage

8 ham hocks
10 pounds fresh collard greens
2 teaspoons salt
1 teaspoon baking soda
1/2 pound fatback (thinly sliced)
1/2 teaspoon crushed red pepper
1 teaspoon black pepper
1 large cabbage

Serves 8 to 10.

Scrub ham hocks thoroughly with a brush under cold running water. Fill a large pot 2/3 full with water, add ham hocks and bring to a boil. Lower heat and simmer until ham hocks are tender when pierced with a fork, about 2 hours.

While ham hocks are cooking: Strip collard greens from stalks. Discard stalks. Fill a large speckled pot with cold water. Add greens, 1 teaspoon salt, and 1 teaspoon baking soda. Soak greens for 30 minutes. *This helps to remove sand and dirt and helps to tenderize greens.* Remove greens from pot and discard water. Wash greens, one leaf at a time, under cold running water. Roll 6 leaves together and slice crosswise into thin strips. Continue until all leaves have been sliced.

When ham hocks are done: Remove from pot with a slotted spoon and set aside. Reserve liquid from pot in a bowl and set aside. *Do not wash pot.* Put fatback in pot and fry over medium heat until fat is rendered. Remove fatback from pot with a slotted spoon and discard. *Do not wash pot. The fat remaining in the pot seasons the greens as they cook.* Add greens, red pepper, remaining salt, and black pepper to pot. Reduce heat, cover and simmer 15 minutes. *As the greens steam they make their own juices.* Add reserved liquid and enough cold water to cover greens. Continue cooking, stirring often. Remove and discard outer, discolored and damaged leaves from cabbage. Cut cabbage head into quarters. Remove and discard core. Slice cabbage. After greens have cooked 1 hour add sliced cabbage and stir well. Cover and cook 45 minutes more. Place ham hocks in pot on top of greens. Cover and continue cooking until done, about 15 minutes more.

Home-Fried Yams and Onions

4 medium-size yams
1/2 pound fatback
1/2 cup sliced onion
1/2 teaspoon salt
1/4 teaspoon pepper
1/8 teaspoon crushed thyme

Serves 4 to 6.

Using a vegetable brush, scrub yams under cold running water. Cut off stems. Put in a large pot and cover with cold water. Bring to a rapid boil. Then lower heat and simmer until tender, approximately 30 minutes. Drain yams, let cool, and peel. Cut each yam into 1/4 -inch thick pieces and set aside. Then cut fatback into thin slices and place in a large iron skillet. Fry until fat is rendered. With a slotted spoon, remove fatback from skillet and discard. *Do not wash skillet.* Put onion in skillet and cook until transparent. Add yams. Sprinkle with salt, pepper, and thyme. Stir several times, until yams are brown. Great with string beans and corn pudding. *(See my recipes.)*

Your Notes:

Mashed Yellow Turnips and Carrots

- *1 large yellow turnip*
- *8 carrots*
- *8 tablespoons butter*
- *1 medium-size onion (diced)*
- *2 teaspoons salt*
- *2 tablespoons sugar*

Serves 8.

Using a vegetable brush, scrub turnip and carrots under cold running water. Peel turnip and cut into medium-size cubes. Peel carrots and cut into 1-inch rounds. Put turnips and carrots in a large pot. Add cold water to cover. Boil until vegetables are tender, about 1 hour. Using a colander, drain off water. Return turnips and carrots to pot and mash with a potato masher. Melt butter in a medium-size iron skillet over low heat. Add onion to skillet and cook until transparent, about 5 minutes. Stir occasionally. *Do not brown.* Add onion, salt, and sugar to pot. Mix well. Serve hot.

Your Notes:

Potato Salad

8 large white potatoes
1/2 cup finely-chopped onion
10 hard boiled eggs (chopped)
1/2 cup finely-diced celery
1/2 cup sweet pickle relish
1 tablespoon sugar
2 teaspoons salt
3/4 cup mayonnaise
1 tablespoon paprika

Serves 6 to 8.

Wash potatoes under cold running water. Place in a large pot and cover with cold water. Boil until potatoes are almost tender when pierced with a fork, about 45 minutes. When potatoes are cooked, remove from pot, let cool and peel. Place in a large bowl, cover and chill in icebox for 1 hour. Dice potatoes and put back into bowl. Add onion, eggs, celery, relish, sugar, salt, and mayonnaise. Mix well with a wooden spoon. Sprinkle with paprika and put back in icebox. Serve chilled. Delicious with pigs' feet.

Your Notes:

Steamed Cabbage

1 (3-pound) cabbage
1 cup cold water
2 chicken bouillon cubes
1 teaspoon caraway seeds

Serves 4 to 6.

Remove and discard any discolored and damaged leaves. Then rinse cabbage. Cut into 8 wedges. Remove and discard core. Pour water into a large pot, put lid on and bring to a boil. Lower heat, add bouillon cubes and stir until dissolved. Add cabbage. Cover and cook 30 minutes over low heat. Remove from heat. Sprinkle caraway seeds on cabbage. Great with pork chops or spare ribs. *(See my recipes.)*

Your Notes:

Stewed Tomatoes

5 cups cold water
12 large tomatoes
3/4 cup sugar
4 slices white bread (toasted)

Serves 6 to 8.

Pour 4 cups cold water into a medium-size pot. Put lid on and bring to a rapid boil. Remove from heat. Stick a fork with a long handle into the stem end of each tomato. Dip each into the hot water and hold there until the skin cracks. *This makes peeling easier.* With a small paring knife, immediately remove and discard skins. Cut tomatoes into quarters and put into a large pot. Add 1 cup cold water and sugar. Put lid on and simmer 30 minutes. Cut toast into cubes and add to pot. Put lid back on and simmer 15 minutes more. Serve hot.

Your Notes:

String Beans and New Potatoes with Smoked Ham Hocks

4 large smoked ham hocks
4 pounds fresh whole string beans
16 small new potatoes

Serves 6 to 8.

Wash ham hocks well under cold running water. Put ham hocks in a large pot and cover with cold water. Bring to a boil. Place lid on pot and simmer until tender, about 2 1/2 hours.

While ham hocks are cooking: Using a colander, wash string beans under cold running water. Remove and discard stems. Leave beans whole. Rinse potatoes under cold running water. Do not peel.

When ham hocks are done: Remove ham hocks with a slotted spoon and set aside. Leave liquid in pot. Add string beans and potatoes to liquid in pot. Cook until potatoes are tender, about 45 minutes. Then put string beans and potatoes in a serving dish. Remove meat from ham hocks and cut into bite-size pieces. Place on top of string beans and potatoes. Serve hot as a main dish.

Most farming families had their own smokehouse. There they smoked meat, such as pig ankles, also known as ham hocks.

Your Notes:

Sunday Turnips with Neck Bones

- 2 *pounds smoked neck bones*
- 6 *cups cold water*
- 1/4 *teaspoon crushed red pepper*
- 2 *teaspoons salt*
- 1 *large onion (peeled, quartered)*
- 8 *pounds white turnips with green tops*
- 1 *teaspoon baking soda*
- 1/2 *teaspoon black pepper*

Serves 6 to 8.

Wash neck bones under cold running water. Put in a large pot and add water. Add red pepper, 1 teaspoon salt, and onion. Cover and bring to a rapid boil. Lower heat and cook 1 1/2 hours.

While meat is cooking: Cut greens from turnips. Fill a large pot with cold water. Add baking soda and remaining salt. Soak greens 30 minutes. *This helps remove any sand and dirt, and helps tenderize the greens.* Remove greens from pot. Put in sink and wash one leaf at a time under cold running water. Roll 6 leaves together and slice cross-wise into thin strips.

When meat is done: Add turnip greens and black pepper to pot. Cover and continue to cook 1 hour longer. Rinse turnips under cold running water, peel and leave whole. Place turnips on top of greens and meat. Cook 30 minutes longer.

Every week the preacher would visit a different family for Sunday supper. He would come to our house the second Sunday of each month. Grandmother would serve fried chicken, rice, corn bread, baked macaroni and cheese, turnips with neck bones, and her delicious coconut cake.

Your Notes:

Zucchini and Yellow Squash

8 medium-size zucchini
8 small yellow squash
6 tablespoons butter
2 teaspoons sugar
1 1/2 teaspoons salt
1/4 teaspoon pepper

Serves 12.

Rinse zucchini and yellow squash under cold running water. Cut vegetables into 1/4 -inch-thick slices. Melt butter over low heat in a large iron skillet. Add vegetables, sugar, salt, and pepper. Stir to blend. Cook 5 minutes, stirring occasionally. Then cover and let simmer 10 minutes.

Southern farms yielded bountiful harvests. During the growing season, our tables were never without fresh vegetables.

Your Notes:

Beans, Grits, Macaroni and Rice

Grandmother would make a large pot of baked beans with a lot of molasses, cinnamon, brown sugar, a few other ingredients and a touch of mustard. When the beans came out of the oven an aroma of cinnamon filled the kitchen.

Baked Macaroni and Cheese

- *1 tablespoon salt*
- *2 tablespoons lard*
- *1 pound uncooked macaroni*
- *4 eggs (lightly beaten)*
- *4 cups milk*
- *1/4 cup grated onion*
- *1/2 pound grated cheddar cheese*
- *6 tablespoons butter*

Serves 8.

Preheat oven to 325° F. Generously butter a 3-quart casserole dish. Fill a large pot with cold water. Add salt and lard. *The lard added to the water prevents macaroni from sticking together.* Bring to a boil. Add macaroni and stir. Cook 15 minutes, stirring often. Drain water and put macaroni in a large bowl. Add eggs, milk, onion, and cheese. Stir macaroni well to blend. Pour into casserole dish and dot with 6 tablespoons butter. Bake 1 hour. Serve hot as a main dish or side dish.

Your Notes:

Black-Eyed Peas and Rice

Grandmother would make a large pot of black-eyed peas and rice. Sometimes she would add ham hocks for seasoning. When they were all ready, she would fix us a large bowl with corn bread and churned butter. Grandfather usually added something hot and spicy to his bowl. Grandmother knew that black-eyed peas, like soup, taste better the second day. So, she always made enough to last for more than one day.

Black-Eyed Peas and Rice

4 large ham hocks (split)
12 cups cold water
3 teaspoons salt
1 teaspoon pepper
1 pound black-eyed peas
1 (8 oz.) can tomato sauce
2½ cups long grain rice

Serves 8.

Wash ham hocks thoroughly under cold running water. Put in a large pot. Add water, salt and pepper. Bring to a brisk boil. Reduce heat to medium and cover. Cook until ham hocks are tender, about 2 hours.

While ham hocks are cooking: Put black-eyed peas in a large bowl and cover with cold water. Using your hand, stir peas several times, and remove and discard discolored or floating ones. Pour off water. Add fresh cold water and soak remaining peas 1 hour. Then drain and set aside.

When ham hocks are done: Remove ham hocks with a slotted spoon and set aside. *Do not throw away liquid. This will season the ingredients.* Put black-eyed peas and tomato sauce in pot. Cover and cook until tender, about 1 hour. Stir in rice. Cover, lower heat and cook 10 minutes. Stir once. Continue cooking 25 minutes longer. Place ham hocks on top of peas and rice and cover. Cook about 10 minutes longer until rice is tender and liquid is absorbed. Delicious with hot corn bread and greens.

In Grandmother's day rice had a coating of talc or glucose which had to be washed off. Washing is no longer necessary or advised, because a lot of nutritional value is lost in the process.

Your Notes:

Country-Style Baked Beans

1 pound northern white navy beans
4 smoked ham hocks (cut in half)
2 teaspoons salt
1 cup ketchup
1/8 teaspoon ground cloves
1 teaspoon dry mustard
1/2 cup dark molasses
1/2 cup firmly-packed light brown sugar
1/4 teaspoon ground cinnamon
1/8 teaspoon ground nutmeg

Serves 8.

Day One: Put beans in a large bowl and cover with cold water. Using your hand, stir beans several times and remove and discard discolored and floating ones. Pour off water. Add fresh cold water and let soak overnight.

Day Two: Drain water from beans. Put beans and ham hocks in a large pot. Cover with cold water. Bring to a brisk boil. Lower heat and cover. Cook for 1 1/2 hours. Remove ham hocks and place in icebox. Preheat oven to 350° F. Remove 2 cups of liquid from pot and set aside. Pour off remaining liquid. In same pot add salt, ketchup, cloves, mustard, molasses, brown sugar, cinnamon, nutmeg, and reserved liquid. Stir to blend. Generously grease a 5-quart casserole dish with butter. Pour in mixture and cover. Bake 60 minutes. Remove cover and continue baking 30 minutes. *Ham hocks can be used to season string beans and greens. (See my recipes.)*

Your Notes:

Cow Peas and Rice

6 corned pig tails
8 cups cold water
1 large onion (coarsely chopped)
3/4 cup cow peas (black-eyed peas can be substituted for cow peas)
2 cups long grain rice
1/4 cup cooking oil

Serves 6.

In a large bowl, soak pig tails 4 hours in lukewarm water. Drain and rinse under cold running water. Put pig tails in a large pot. Add water and chopped onion and bring to a brisk boil. Lower heat, cover and simmer 2 hours.

While pig tails are cooking: Pour peas into a large bowl and cover with cold water. Using your hand, stir peas several times, and remove and discard discolored or floating ones. Pour off water. Add fresh cold water and soak peas 1 hour. Then drain and set aside.

When pig tails are done: Add peas to pot. Cover and cook about 1 hour more. Remove pig tails from pot with a slotted spoon and set aside. Add rice and oil to pot and stir. Bring to a rapid boil. Lower heat and cover. After rice has cooked 35 minutes, put pig tails on top of mixture and cover. Continue cooking about 10 minutes more, until rice is tender and liquid is completely absorbed. Stir to fluff. Serve hot with greens. *(See my recipes.)*

Your Notes:

Grits Soufflé

- *4 cups cold water*
- *1 teaspoon salt*
- *1 cup old-fashioned grits*
- *6 tablespoons butter*
- *3 tablespoons all-purpose flour*
- *2 teaspoons dry mustard*
- *3 eggs (separated)*
- *2 cups grated cheddar cheese*

Serves 8.

Separate eggs while they are cold. Crack each egg and separate whites into one small bowl and yolks into a second bowl.

Preheat oven to 350º F. Grease a 2-quart casserole dish with lard. Pour water into a 2-quart saucepot, add salt and bring to a boil. Reduce heat and slowly stir in grits. Stir frequently until grits begin to thicken. Cover and continue cooking for 20 minutes. Melt butter in a small saucepot over low heat. Stir in flour and mustard. Cook 5 minutes. In a small bowl, combine egg yolks, butter mixture and cheese. Stir to blend. When grits are done, add egg mixture slowly, while stirring constantly until blended. Beat egg whites until stiff. Fold into grits. Pour mixture into casserole dish. Bake 45 minutes. Serve alone, or as a side dish.

Your Notes:

Hominy Grits

4 cups water
1 1/2 teaspoons salt
1 cup old-fashioned grits
1/4 cup butter

Serves 4 to 6.

Pour water into a 2-quart pot and add salt. Bring to a boil. Reduce heat and slowly stir in grits. Cook over low heat 45 minutes. Stir often to prevent lumping. Serve with butter.

Hominy Grits with Mild Cheddar Cheese: Follow the recipe for hominy grits. After grits are cooked, add 3/4 cup grated mild cheddar cheese. Stir until cheese melts.

Fried Grits: Follow the recipe for hominy grits. Pour grits into a 9x5x2-inch loaf pan. Cover and place in icebox overnight. Remove from loaf pan and slice into 1/2 -inch thick pieces. Melt 1/2 cup of lard in a large iron skillet over medium heat. When lard is hot, add grits. Fry on both sides until brown.

All of the above can be served as a main dish, or as a side.

Your Notes:

Meats, Poultry and Seafood

I remember helping Grandmother prepare our holiday turkey. She plucked the feathers, washed, buttered, and seasoned it. Then she made the stuffing. When the turkey was done, Grandmother would place it on the table with all the other delicious foods. Grandfather would say the blessing, thankful for Grandmother, me and my brother, my cousins, our neighbors, friends, and all the blessings bestowed upon our home. Then he carved and served the turkey.

Baked Country-Smoked Ham

1 (8 to 10-pound) smoked ham
1 (16 oz.) jar pineapple slices
2 cups apple cider, or apple juice
1 cup firmly-packed light brown sugar

Serves 12 to 15.

Day One: Put ham in a large pot. Cover with water and soak 5 hours in icebox. Pour off water. Cover with fresh cold water and soak overnight in icebox.

Day Two: Pour off water. Cover ham with fresh cold water. Boil 3 hours and drain. Put ham in a large roasting pan and let cool. Lift up edges of skin with a sharp knife. Gently pull skin off and discard. Preheat oven to 325° F. Place pineapple slices on ham and use toothpicks to hold them in place. Pat on brown sugar. Combine pineapple juice with cider and pour into bottom of pan. Bake 2 hours, basting every 30 minutes. Delicious hot or cold with any meal.

Grandfather would remove several pieces of straw from a broom and wash them to use as toothpicks. They would be kept in a jar on the kitchen counter, or in the cupboard.

Your Notes:

Baked Virginia Ham

1 (8 to 10-pound) Virginia ham

2 cups warmed apricot preserves

Serves 12 to 15.

Virginia ham is quite salty. Soak in cold water for at least 24 hours in icebox. The water should be changed every 8 hours. Place ham in a large pot. Cover with fresh cold water. Bring to a boil. Lower heat and simmer 4 to 6 hours, *or* until tender when pierced with a fork *(start checking after 3 hours).* Preheat oven to 350º F. Place ham in a large roasting pan. Lift up edges of skin with a sharp knife. Gently pull skin off and discard. Score ham fat. Spoon 1 cup of preserves over ham. Place in oven. Bake 45 minutes, basting every 15 minutes using drippings and remaining preserves. Bake until ham is golden brown. Serve with cheese biscuits, potato salad and collard greens. *(See my recipes.)*

A large deep tin tub was used to soak hams. The large speckled roasting pan was a perfect fit for roasting the ham.

Your Notes:

Barbecued Breast of Lamb

6 racks breast of lamb

2 cups barbecue sauce (See my recipes.)

Serves 6 to 12.

Have butcher cut breast of lamb through the bony part, about 2 inches apart.

On the Grill: Wash lamb thoroughly under cold running water. Pat dry thoroughly and place on grill with the bony side down. Keep sauce warm on grill while barbecuing. Brush meat on both sides with barbecue sauce. Turn over and baste every 15 minutes. Barbecue 1 hour 30 minutes, *or* until tender when pierced with a fork. When meat is ready to serve, brush with remaining sauce. Serve with corn bread, potato salad and greens. *(See my recipes.)*

Oven Baked: Wash lamb thoroughly under cold running water. Pat dry thoroughly. Pre-heat oven to 350°F. Put a small amount of barbecue sauce in a shallow baking pan. Place lamb in pan and brush on barbecue sauce. Baste every 15 minutes. Bake 1 hour 30 minutes, *or* until tender when pierced with a fork.

Preparing the grill:

Light a mound of wood. When the wood burns down into coals, spread some out creating a warm cooking area, keeping the remainder in a hot mound. Place meat high enough over coals so the drippings don't cause flare-ups. Allow coals to burn for 20 to 30 minutes before barbecuing. Coals will appear ash grey in daylight and glow red at night. For coals to burn properly, tap often to loosen the ash. If you can hold your hands, palms down, over the coals for a second or two, the coals are hot; three seconds, they are medium-hot; four seconds, they are medium; five seconds, they are warming coals.

Barbecued Chicken

3	*whole fryer chickens*	2	*cups barbecue sauce (See my recipes.)*
3	*teaspoons salt*		

Serves 6 to 8.

On the Grill: *(See page 83, Preparing the grill.)* Wash chickens thoroughly, inside and outside, under cold running water. Pat dry thoroughly. Cut chickens into serving pieces *(see page 92 for instructions)* and season with salt. Place on grill. Brush both sides with barbecue sauce. Turn over every 15 minutes and brush on barbecue sauce. Cook 45 to 60 minutes, *or* until tender when pierced with a fork.

Oven Baked: Leave chickens whole. Clean and season chickens as above. Preheat oven to 350º F. Put a small amount of barbecue sauce in shallow baking pans. Place chickens in pans and brush on barbecue sauce. Baste every 15 minutes. Bake 1 hour, *or* until tender when pierced with a fork. Remove from oven and cut into serving pieces *(see page 92 for instructions).* Good with baked peach halves. *(See my recipe.)*

My Grandmother would catch a chicken, wring its neck, then cut off its head. She would pluck the feathers using a sharp knife, and singe off remaining fine hairs. Then she cleaned and prepared it for supper. The feet would be saved and used for making soup.

Your Notes:

Barbecued Ribs

3	*slabs spareribs (about 6 pounds total)*	*4*	*tablespoons salt*
1/2	*cup vinegar*	*2*	*cups barbecue sauce (See my recipes.)*

Serves 8 to 12.

On the Grill: *(See page 83, Preparing the grill.)* Rinse ribs under cold running water. Pat dry and cut, *or* pull off, excess fat. Cut each slab between the ribs into 3 pieces. Place in a large pot and cover with cold water. Add vinegar and salt. Boil 45 minutes. Pour off water and pat ribs dry. Place ribs on grill. Brush both sides with barbecue sauce. Turn ribs over once and brush on additional sauce. Cook about 20 minutes, *or* until tender when pierced with a fork. Remove from grill and cut into individual servings. Serve hot with fried fresh corn, potato salad and greens. *(See my recipes.)*

Oven Baked: Preheat oven to 325° F. Rinse ribs under cold running water. Pat dry and cut, *or* pull off, excess fat. Put a small amount of barbecue sauce in shallow baking pans. Place spareribs in pans and brush on barbecue sauce. Turn ribs over and baste every 15 minutes. Bake approximately 2 hours, *or* until tender when pierced with a fork. Remove from oven and cut into individual servings.

When Grandfather barbecued, he dug a large hole and lined the bottom with rocks. He arranged wood in a mound, then lit it. When the fire was hot, he spread some of the wood out to create a warm area. He left the remainder in a hot mound.

Your Notes:

Barbecued Turkey Wings

12 turkey wings

3 cups barbecue sauce (See my recipes.)

Serves 6.

On the Grill: *(See page 83, Preparing the grill.)* Remove and discard any pin feathers from turkey wings. Rinse wings thoroughly under cold running water. Pat dry and place on grill. Brush both sides with barbecue sauce. Approximately every 15 minutes turn wings over and brush generously with additional sauce. Cook 1 hour 30 minutes, *or* until meat is tender when pierced with a fork. Use remaining sauce over meat when served.

Oven Baked: Clean turkey wings as above. Preheat oven to 350º F. Put a small amount of barbecue sauce in a shallow baking pan. Place wings in pan and brush on barbecue sauce. Turn wings over and baste every 15 minutes. Bake 1 hour, *or* until tender when pierced with a fork. Good with fresh baked peach halves. *(See my recipe.)*

Your Notes:

Boiled Fresh Pig Feet

12 whole fresh pig feet
1 cup white vinegar
2 large onions (peeled, cut in half)
2 teaspoons crushed red pepper
4 tablespoons salt

Serves 6 to 8.

Using a kitchen brush with strong bristles, scrub and wash pig feet under cold running water. With a sharp knife, cut away and discard hair between toes. Put pig feet into a large pot and cover with cold water. Add vinegar, onion, red pepper, and salt. Cover and bring to a boil. Lower heat and cook 3 hours. Using a slotted spoon, remove pig feet and place on a large platter. Serve hot. Delicious with collard greens or turnip greens. *(See my recipes.)*

Your Notes:

Chicken Corn Casserole

- 4 *tablespoons butter*
- 4 *tablespoons flour*
- 1 *cup milk*
- 1 *cup chicken broth*
- 3 *eggs*
- 1 1/2 *cups diced cooked chicken*
- 1 *cup whole kernel corn*
- 2 *tablespoons diced pimiento*
- 1 *teaspoon salt*
- 1/8 *teaspoon cayenne pepper*

Serves 4 to 6.

Preheat oven to 325° F. Generously grease a 2 1/2-quart casserole dish with lard. Over low heat, melt butter in a large saucepot. Slowly stir in flour with a wooden spoon until well blended. Gradually stir milk and broth into butter mixture. Continue cooking and stirring 5 minutes, *or* until mixture thickens forming a sauce. Remove from heat. Beat eggs in a small bowl. Slowly stir 1/4 cup sauce into eggs. Then slowly stir egg mixture into sauce in pot. Add chicken, corn, pimiento, salt, and cayenne pepper. Stir to mix. Pour mixture into casserole dish. Bake 30 minutes, *or* until a knife inserted into the center comes out clean. Serve hot. Great with biscuits. *(See my recipes.)*

Your Notes:

Chicken'n Dumplings

- *1 large stewing chicken*
- *8 cups cold water*
- *3 chicken bouillon cubes*
- *1 cup sliced celery*
- *1 cup chopped onion*
- *1/4 cup chopped fresh parsley*

Serves 6 to 8.

Wash chicken thoroughly, inside and outside, under cold running water. Pat dry. Cut into serving pieces *(see page 92 for instructions)* and put into a large pot. Add water, bouillon cubes, celery, onion, and parsley. Cover pot and bring to a boil. Lower heat and simmer 1 hour. After 45 minutes, begin preparing dumplings.

Dumplings:

- *1 1/2 cups sifted all-purpose flour*
- *2 teaspoons baking powder*
- *1 teaspoon salt*
- *1/3 cup lard*
- *2/3 cup milk*

In a sifter, combine flour, baking powder, and salt. Sift into a medium-size bowl. Add lard. Cut lard into flour mixture with a fork until mixture is crumbly. Slowly stir in milk and mix until dough is smooth. Immediately scoop and drop rounded tablespoons of dough directly into pot with chicken and bring to a boil. Cover pot and lower heat. Simmer 20 minutes more. *Do not remove lid until cooking time is completed.*

Grandmother raised fryers which usually had white or black feathers.
Mrs. Scruggs raised stewing chickens which had red feathers.
Roosters were also used as stewing chickens.

Chit'lings

When it came time to prepare chit'lings, Mrs. Scruggs, a long-time friend and neighbor, would come over to help Grandmother. They would send me and Mrs. Scruggs' daughter Cathy to get three or four long thin branches from a nearby tree. Cathy and I stripped off all the leaves. Then Grandmother scraped off all the bark until the sticks were clean and white. Grandmother showed us how to put a branch in the end of the chit'lings to turn them inside out for cleaning. The grown-ups took care of the rest.

Chit'lings (Chitterlings)

20 pounds fresh chit'lings
2 cups white vinegar
2 tablespoons crushed red pepper
4 tablespoons hot pepper sauce
2 large onions (peeled)
4 tablespoons salt

Serves 6 to 8.

Wash chit'lings thoroughly under cold running water. *It is important that chit'lings are cleaned extremely well.* Use the handle of a wooden spoon to push one end of chit'lings through the other end, turning them inside out. Pull off and discard excess fat. Wash chit'lings thoroughly, *several times*, under cold running water. Turn right side out. Put chit'lings in a large pot. Cover with cold water, add 1 cup vinegar, and soak 1 hour. Drain chit'lings, return to pot and cover with cold water. Add remaining vinegar, red pepper, hot pepper sauce, onions, and salt. Bring to a boil. Then lower heat. Cover pot and simmer until tender, about 3 hours. Reserve 2 cups of liquid from pot. Drain chit'lings in a colander and discard onions. Cut chit'lings into bite-size pieces. Put reserved liquid and chit'lings back into pot. Re-heat. Serve hot with collard greens and potato salad. *(See my recipes.)*

Virtually every part of the pig was used -- skin, fat, feet, ankles, ears, head, and small intestines (chit'lings).

Your Notes:

Fried Chicken

- *1 (3 1/2-pound) fryer chicken*
- *1/2 cup flour*
- *1 teaspoon salt*
- *1/2 teaspoon pepper*
- *1 cup lard*
- *1/4 cup butter*

Serves 4 to 6.

Day One: Wash chicken, inside and outside, under cold running water and pat dry. Cut into serving pieces. In a brown paper bag, combine chicken, salt, and pepper. Shake to mix. Put chicken on platter, cover and place in icebox overnight.

Day Two: Put chicken and flour in a brown paper bag and shake to coat. In a large iron skillet, melt lard and butter together over medium heat. Keep oil hot while frying. For best results, cook only a few pieces at a time. *Too many pieces at one time will make the temperature of the lard too low.* Add chicken, skin side down. Fry until golden brown, about five minutes. Turn chicken over, cover and cook about 45 minutes longer. Remove chicken and drain on brown paper to absorb excess fat. ***For crispier chicken:*** *Remove cover for last 10 minutes of cooking.*

How to cut a chicken into serving pieces:
Clean chicken thoroughly, inside and outside, and pat dry. ***Removing the wings:*** Cut the skin where the wing meets the body. Bend the wing back until the joint breaks. Cut off the wing. ***Removing the thighs:*** Pull the leg and thigh away from the body and cut the skin where the thigh meets the body. With one hand holding the body, bend the thigh back until the bone pops out of the hip joint and you can see the bone. At the joint, cut as close to the backbone as possible, cutting the thigh away from the body. ***Removing the drumsticks:*** Bend back the joint between the thigh and drumstick until it pops. Cut off the drumstick at the joint. ***Removing the breasts:*** Starting at the neck, cut lengthwise through the breast bone and backbone. ***Removing the backbone:*** Cut the backbone away from breast bone.

Fried Country Ham with Red-Eye Gravy

4 tablespoons lard
4 slices cured country ham (cut into halves)
2 tablespoons all-purpose flour
1 1/2 cups cold water
2 tablespoons fresh brewed coffee

Serves 4 to 8.

Over medium heat, melt lard in a large iron skillet. Put ham in skillet. Fry until lightly browned on both sides. Remove from skillet and place on a platter. Sprinkle flour into lard in skillet and stir until smooth. Gradually add water to create gravy, stirring constantly until slightly thickened. Add coffee and stir. Put ham in gravy. Cook 5 minutes. Serve hot. Delicious with biscuits and grits. *(See my recipes.)*

Ham was sliced with the bone in it. The bone, with its red marrow, resembles an eye; hence, the name 'red-eye'.

Your Notes:

Fried Rabbit

- *4 rabbits (skinned, gutted)*
- *1 cup white vinegar*
- *1 tablespoon crushed red pepper*
- *2 cups lard*
- *1 1/2 cups all-purpose flour*
- *1 tablespoon salt*
- *1 tablespoon black pepper*

Serves 8.

Remove head and feet from rabbits. Thoroughly clean rabbits under cold running water. Cut each rabbit into quarters. Place in a large pot and cover with water. Add vinegar and red pepper. Bring to a rapid boil. Reduce heat and cook 1 hour. Remove rabbit from pot, pat dry and set aside. Combine flour, salt, and black pepper in a brown paper bag and shake to mix. Put rabbit, a few pieces at a time, in bag and shake to coat. In a large iron skillet, melt lard over medium-high heat. Keep oil hot while frying. For best results, cook only a few pieces at a time. *Too many pieces at one time will make the temperature of the lard too low.* Place rabbit in skillet and fry until golden brown, about 5 minutes, turning once. Place on brown paper to absorb excess fat. Serve with greens and corn bread. *(See my recipes.)*

Your Notes:

Iron-Skillet Baked Pot Roast

1 (5 to 7-pound) rump of beef
1/2 cup butter (room temperature)
1 cup cold water
2 cups coarsely-chopped onion
1 cup sliced celery
2 cups finely-chopped tomatoes
8 medium-size white potatoes
8 small carrots
3 teaspoons salt

Serves 8 to 12.

Preheat oven to 350° F. Wipe roast with a damp towel. Rub butter on entire roast. Place roast in a deep iron skillet. Add water, onion, celery, and tomatoes. Cover and bake 3 hours. While meat is cooking, wash and peel potatoes *(leave whole)*. Put potatoes in a bowl, cover with cold water and place in icebox until ready to use. *This keeps potatoes from turning dark.* Wash carrots, cut into halves and set aside. After 3 hours remove roast from oven. Place potatoes and carrots around roast. Sprinkle on salt and cook uncovered 1 hour longer. Good with hot buttermilk rolls. *(See my recipe.)*

Your Notes:

Pork Chops Smothered with Onions

- 6 *pork chops*
- 2 *teaspoons pepper*
- 1/4 *cup lard*
- 1/4 *cup butter*
- 2 *cups sliced onion*
- 3/4 *cup water*
- 2 *chicken bouillon cubes*

Serves 6.

Rinse chops under cold running water and pat dry. Sprinkle with pepper. Melt lard and butter together in a large iron skillet over medium heat. Fry chops until brown on both sides. Crush bouillon cubes and add to skillet. Then add onion and water. Lower heat, cover, and simmer 1 hour. Serve with fried apples, biscuits and grits. *(See my recipes.)*

Your Notes:

Potted Chicken Wings

- *1 pound whole okra*
- *16 chicken wings*
- *6 tablespoons lard*
- *2 tablespoons butter*
- *2 cups chopped onions*
- *1 (16 oz.) jar whole tomatoes*
- *1 (16 oz.) jar whole kernel corn*
- *3 cups chicken broth*
- *2 teaspoons salt*
- *1 teaspoon pepper*
- *1 tablespoon paprika*
- *1/4 cup all-purpose flour*
- *1/4 cup cold water*

Serves 4 to 6.

Wash okra in a colander under cold running water. Cut off and discard tops and bottoms. Set okra aside. Wash chicken wings thoroughly under cold running water. Remove and discard all pin feathers. Melt lard and butter together in a large iron pot over medium heat. Lightly brown chicken wings on both sides. Lower heat and add onions. Cook about 10 minutes, stirring occasionally. Add tomatoes, corn, chicken broth, salt, pepper, and paprika. Stir to mix. Cover and simmer 30 minutes. Combine flour and water in a small bowl. Stir to make a smooth paste. Gradually stir flour mixture into pot. Continue stirring until mixture begins to thicken. Stir okra into mixture. Cover and simmer 25 minutes more, *or* until tender.

Your Notes:

Roast Loin of Pork with Gravy

1	*(6-pound) loin of pork*	*2*	*cups cold water*
6	*tablespoons all-purpose flour*	*1*	*cup coarsely-chopped onion*
2	*chicken bouillon cubes*	*2*	*tablespoons butter*

Serves 6 to 8.

Preheat oven to 325° F. Rinse pork under cold running water and pat dry. Lightly dust pork with 4 tablespoons flour. Place in a large baking pan. Crumble bouillon cubes around pork. Add water, onion, and butter. Cover and bake 2 hours. Remove cover and continue baking until browned, about 1 hour longer. Place pork on a serving platter. Serve with homemade applesauce. *(See my recipe.)*

To make gravy: Pour all drippings from roasting pan into a large glass measuring cup. Allow to stand until fat floats to the top. Return 2 tablespoons of fat to roasting pan. Remove and discard remaining fat from measuring cup. Return drippings to pan. Place roasting pan on top of stove over low heat. Using a spoon, stir and scrape sides and bottom of pan to loosen browned drippings. To prevent lumping, sprinkle remaining flour slowly into roasting pan while stirring with a fork until mixture is smooth. Simmer 5 minutes, stirring frequently, until thickened. Pour into a serving bowl.

Your Notes:

Roast Turkey

- *stuffing (See my recipes.)*
- *1 (12 to 15-pound) turkey*
- *2 teaspoons salt*
- *1 teaspoon black pepper*
- *1/2 cup butter*
- *2 cups water*
- *2 bouillon cubes*

Serves 8 to 10.

Prepare stuffing and set aside. Preheat oven to 325° F. Remove giblets and neck from cavity of turkey and set aside. Wash turkey thoroughly inside and outside. Pat dry. Combine salt and pepper in a small bowl. Sprinkle half of salt mixture inside turkey cavity. Rub remaining mixture on outside of turkey. Then stuff neck cavity. Smooth neck skin over stuffing and skewer to back of turkey. Stuff body cavity. *Do not pack the stuffing tightly -- it needs room to expand as it cooks.* Close opening by sewing loosely with white thread. Cross legs and wrap white thread around legs to hold in place. (*If turkey legs are tucked under band-like skin, slip legs out, stuff lightly and slip legs back into place.)* Place turkey on a rack in a large roasting pan. Cover with double-folded cheesecloth. Melt butter over low heat in a small saucepot and drizzle over turkey. Add water and bouillon cubes to bottom of pan. Place in oven and bake 3 1/2 to 4 1/2 hours. Baste every 30 minutes. Remove cheesecloth after 3 hours of cooking. Begin testing for doneness after 3 1/2 hours. (*Snip thread from legs and move drumstick up and down. It should twist easily.)* When turkey is done, place on a warm platter. Snip and discard remaining thread. Remove stuffing and place in a serving bowl. Use drippings to make gravy. (*See my recipe, page 123.)*

Your Notes:

Crabbing

Grandfather, Mr. Thomas and Mr. Scruggs went crabbing regularly during the season. They would go to a special place. Usually it would take all day for them to catch enough for dinner.

Batter-Fried Soft-Shell Crabs

18 live soft-shell crabs
3/4 cup all-purpose flour
2 teaspoons salt
1 teaspoon pepper
1 1/4 cups cold water
8 tablespoons butter
1 cup lard

Serves 9.

Preparation of crabs: Rinse live crabs under cold running water. Place each crab on a cutting board with its back up. Cut off the head 1/2 to 3/4 inch behind the eyes. Pull back the pointed ends of the crab's back about halfway. Then scrape out and discard the spongy material. Turn crab over. Pull off and discard the tail *(apron)* which folds under the crab. Remove and discard the spongy mass under the tail. Rinse crabs quickly under cold running water. Drain, pat dry and set aside.

Combine flour, salt, and pepper in a medium-size bowl. Add water and stir to create a smooth thin batter. Melt butter and lard in a deep iron skillet over medium heat until hot. Dip each crab in batter to coat it. Fry 3 or 4 crabs at a time, turning once. Cook until golden brown on both sides, 2 to 3 minutes. Remove crabs from skillet and place on brown paper to absorb fat. Serve hot. *The entire cooked crab is edible.*

Your Notes:

Boiled Hard-Shell Crabs

6 tablespoons Old Bay Seasoning
1 (12 oz.) can cola
18 live hard-shell blue crabs

Serves 4 to 6.

Fill a 12-quart pot 2/3 full with cold water. Add seasoning and cola. Cover and bring to a brisk boil. Using long tongs, quickly put all crabs, head first, into pot. Put lid back on and bring to a second boil. Boil about 20 minutes. Crabs will be pink when done. Drain off water. Quickly cover crabs with cold water until slightly cooled, about 1 minute, and drain again. Place on a platter and serve immediately.

Grandmother had clean hairpins set aside in the cupboard. She and Grandfather would use them to pull the meat out of the crabs for all of us.

Your Notes:

Crab Cakes

4 slices white bread
1 egg
1/4 cup mayonnaise
1 teaspoon mustard
1 teaspoon Worcestershire sauce
2 tablespoons parsley
1 teaspoon paprika
1/2 teaspoon cayenne pepper
1 pound crabmeat (cleaned)
1/2 cup lard
1/4 cup butter

Makes 6 crab cakes.

Lightly toast bread on both sides. Place on table to dry out, about 30 minutes. Do not stack bread. Using a rolling pin, roll over the bread several times, to make crumbs. In a large bowl combine bread crumbs, egg, mayonnaise, mustard, Worcestershire sauce, parsley, paprika, and cayenne pepper. Mix well. Then gently mix in crabmeat. If mixture is too dry, add more mayonnaise. Divide mixture into 6 portions. Using your hands shape into cakes. In a large skillet heat lard and butter until hot. Fry crab cakes 5 minutes. Using a slotted spoon, turn over and fry 5 minutes more. Place crab cakes on brown paper to absorb excess fat.

Your Notes:

Fishing

When Grandmother wanted fish for dinner, Grandfather would take his bamboo pole, head for the pond, and catch a big batch of catfish. He would clean them and remove the bones. Grandmother would fry hush puppies to go along with the fish. What a meal!

Fried Catfish Fillets

8 fresh catfish fillets
2 teaspoons salt
2 teaspoons pepper
1 cup white cornmeal
1 1/2 cups lard

Serves 4 to 6.

Day One: Rinse fillets under cold running water, pat dry and put on a plate. Combine salt, pepper, and cornmeal in a small bowl and stir to mix. Generously sprinkle cornmeal mixture over both sides of fillets. Place in icebox overnight.

Day Two: Melt lard in a large iron skillet over high heat. Keep oil hot while frying. For best results, cook only a few fillets at a time. *Too many at one time will make the temperature of the lard too low.* Fry fillets on both sides until golden brown. Place on brown paper to absorb excess fat. Serve with hush puppies. *(See my recipe.)*

How to clean and fillet fresh catfish: Rinse catfish under cold running water and pat dry. Lay fish on its side. Use a sharp knife. Cut around the base of the fins. Remove and discard fins and fin bones. Make a shallow cut all the way around the head and behind the gills. Then pull the skin back over the tail. Cut off and discard head and tail. Then cut lengthwise along the belly. Remove and discard entrails. Next, start at head end of catfish and cut to tail end along one side of the backbone. Continue cutting in this manner, head to tail. Keep the knife flat against the bones, until the flesh is completely separated from the bones. Repeat on the other side. This will result in two fillets. Remove and discard all bones. Rinse fillets under cold running water and pat dry.

Early Friday mornings the fishman would drive his horse and cart through the neighborhood yelling, "Fishman! Fishman!" My grandmother would go out and choose what she wanted. Then he would weigh and clean it, then wrap it in newspaper.

Fried Mullets and Roe

8	*mullet fillets*	*2*	*teaspoons pepper*
4	*mullet roe*	*1 1/2*	*cups white cornmeal*
2	*teaspoons salt*	*1 1/2*	*cups lard*

Serves 4 to 6.

Day One: Rinse fillets and roe under cold running water, pat dry and put on a plate. Combine salt, pepper, and cornmeal in a small bowl and stir to mix. Generously sprinkle cornmeal mixture over both sides of fillets. Roll roe in remaining cornmeal. Store in icebox overnight.

Day Two: Melt lard in a large iron skillet over high heat. Keep oil hot while frying. For best results, cook only a few fillets at a time. *Too many at one time will make the temperature of the lard too low.* Fry fillets on both sides until golden brown. Place fillets on a brown paper bag to absorb excess fat. Then fry roe until golden brown. *Watch carefully to avoid burning.* Delicious with corn bread. *(See my recipes.)*

How to clean and fillet fresh mullet:
Rinse fish under cold running water and pat dry. Scale fish by scraping backwards from tail to head. Use a sharp knife to carefully cut just the skin lengthwise along the belly to expose the roe (an orange sack of fish eggs). *Be careful not to make a deep cut which could damage the roe.* Remove roe and set aside. Remove and discard entrails. Cut around fins to remove fins and fin bones. Cut off the head. Cut lengthwise head to tail along one side of the backbone. Continue cutting in this manner, peeling the skin back as you cut from head to tail. Keep the knife flat against the bones, until the flesh is completely separated from the bones. Repeat on the other side. This will result in two fillets. Remove and discard all bones. Rinse fillets under cold running water and pat dry.

Grandmother would place a brown paper bag in the sink.
Then she placed one fish at a time on the bag and scraped off the
scales with a spoon. The spoon kept the scales from flying all over.

Steamed Live Crabs

- *8 cups cold water*
- *1/2 cup white vinegar*
- *4 rounded tablespoons Old Bay Seasoning, or Crab Boil*
- *1 teaspoon black pepper*
- *1 teaspoon crushed red pepper*
- *36 live hard-shell crabs*

Serves 12 to 18.

Pour water into a large pot, *or* a crab kettle. Add vinegar, Old Bay Seasoning, black pepper, and red pepper. *Repeat the following process for each batch* (approximately 12 crabs): Bring to a rapid boil. Using long tongs, quickly put crabs, head first, into pot. Put lid on and steam 15 to 20 minutes, *or* until crabs have turned a reddish pink. Turn heat off. Immediately remove crabs from pot using long tongs. Serve hot.

Optional: Add a 12 oz. cola, *or* a 12 oz. beer to water in pot.

Your Notes:

Relishes, Sauces, Gravies and Stuffings

The holiday table was not complete without fresh cranberry sauce with pecans and giblet gravy to dip homemade breads and rolls in.

Barbecue Sauce ~ Country-Style

1 cup white vinegar
1/2 cup water
4 tablespoons molasses
1/4 cup Worcestershire sauce
3 teaspoons salt
1 teaspoon onion powder
1/2 teaspoon Tabasco sauce
1/2 cup cooking oil

Makes 1 1/2 cups.

In a 1-quart pot, combine vinegar, water, molasses, Worcestershire sauce, salt, onion powder, Tabasco sauce, and oil. Stir to blend. Simmer uncovered 30 minutes, stirring occasionally.

Your Notes:

Barbecue Sauce ~ Spicy and Hot

- *2 teaspoons hot pepper sauce*
- *2 tablespoons prepared mustard*
- *1 cup hot chili sauce*
- *3 tablespoons Worcestershire sauce*
- *1/2 cup finely-chopped onion*
- *3 teaspoons salt*
- *3 tablespoons firmly-packed brown sugar*
- *3/4 cup water*
- *1/2 cup lard*
- *1/3 cup orange juice*

Makes 2 cups.

In a saucepan, combine hot pepper sauce, mustard, chili sauce, Worcestershire sauce, onion, salt, brown sugar, water, lard, and orange juice. Stir well to blend. Simmer 20 minutes, stirring occasionally.

Your Notes:

Barbecue Sauce ~ Zesty

1 cup ketchup
1 cup chili sauce
1/4 cup prepared dry mustard
3/4 cup firmly-packed light brown sugar
4 tablespoons fresh lemon juice
1/4 cup steak sauce
2 tablespoons Worcestershire sauce
1 tablespoon cooking oil
1 cup beer
2 drops liquid smoke

Makes about 2 1/2 cups.

In a medium-size saucepan combine ketchup, chili sauce, mustard, brown sugar, lemon juice, steak sauce, Worcestershire sauce, oil, and beer. Simmer uncovered over low heat 15 minutes, stirring occasionally. Remove from heat and stir in liquid smoke.

Your Notes:

Corn Bread Stuffing

8 slices toast (cubed)
4 cups crumbled corn bread
2 tablespoons chopped parsley
1 1/2 teaspoons sage
1/2 cup butter
1 cup diced celery
1 cup chopped onion
2 eggs (lightly beaten)
1 cup chicken broth
2 teaspoons salt
1 teaspoon pepper

Stuffs one 12 to 18-pound bird.

In a large bowl, combine toast, corn bread, parsley, and sage. Mix well. In a large iron skillet, melt butter over medium heat. Put celery and onion in skillet and stir. Cook 5 minutes. Let cool and add to dry ingredients. Then add eggs, chicken broth, salt, and pepper. Mix well. Place in icebox until completely cooled. Stuff bird loosely. (Stuffing needs room to expand as it cooks.) Seal cavity with skewers, or sew closed with white thread. *Do not stuff bird until just before cooking.*

Your Notes:

Cranberry Chutney

- *1 pound fresh cranberries*
- *1/2 cup cold water*
- *1 cup peeled, diced green apples*
- *2 cups sugar*
- *1/2 cup vinegar*
- *1/4 cup chopped mixed candied fruit*
- *1/2 teaspoon salt*
- *1/4 teaspoon ground ginger*
- *1/8 teaspoon ground cloves*
- *1/4 teaspoon ground allspice*
- *1/4 teaspoon dry mustard*
- *1/2 cup finely-chopped walnuts*

Makes 4 cups.

Put cranberries in a colander. Discard any bad ones. Remove stems and rinse cranberries under cold running water. Put cranberries in a 3-quart saucepan. Add water, apples, sugar, vinegar, candied fruit, salt, ginger, cloves, allspice, and mustard. Mix well and bring to a boil. Reduce heat. Simmer 15 minutes, stirring occasionally to prevent burning. Remove from heat. Stir in walnuts and let cool. Place in icebox until ready to serve. Serve with ham, turkey or chicken. *(See my recipes.)*

Your Notes:

Fried Green Apples

3/4 pound salt pork
8 large tart green apples
1/2 cup sugar
3/4 cup firmly-packed light brown sugar
1/4 cup lemon juice

Serves 6.

Thinly slice salt pork. Fry salt pork in a large iron skillet over medium heat until fat is rendered. Remove salt pork from skillet with a slotted spoon and place on brown paper to absorb excess fat. *(Cooked salt pork makes a good snack.)* Set skillet aside with rendered fat. Wash apples under cold running water. *Do not peel apples.* Core apples and remove all seeds. Slice into thin pieces and put in a medium-size bowl. Add lemon juice and stir, making sure that all slices are well coated. Put apples in skillet and put lid on. Simmer over low heat until apples are tender, about 20 minutes. Stir often while apples are simmering. Remove lid and stir in sugar and brown sugar. Continue cooking and stirring until sugar is melted and apples are light brown. Serve with pork chops. *(See my recipes.)*

During apple season, fried green apples were served with most meals and as a snack. This dish usually was found on the table at family get-togethers and church dinners.

Your Notes:

Homemade Applesauce

8 large McIntosh apples
1 cup cold water
2 tablespoons lemon juice
2 teaspoons ground cinnamon
1 teaspoon ground nutmeg
3/4 cup firmly-packed light brown sugar

Serves 6 to 8.

Wash apples under cold running water. *Do not peel or remove seeds*. Cut into quarters and place in a large saucepot with water and lemon juice. Bring to a boil. Lower heat and cover. Simmer about 30 minutes. Stir in cinnamon, nutmeg, and brown sugar. Continue simmering 15 minutes more. Place a sieve over a medium-size bowl. Press apples through sieve using a wooden spoon. Discard seeds and skins. Stir applesauce. Delicious warm or cold.

Your Notes:

Stuffing

I helped Grandmother make stuffing. I would toast the bread, cut up the vegetables, melt the butter, and add the seasonings. I loved the smell of the mixture when stirring it all together. After it had cooled, she would stuff the turkey or chickens.

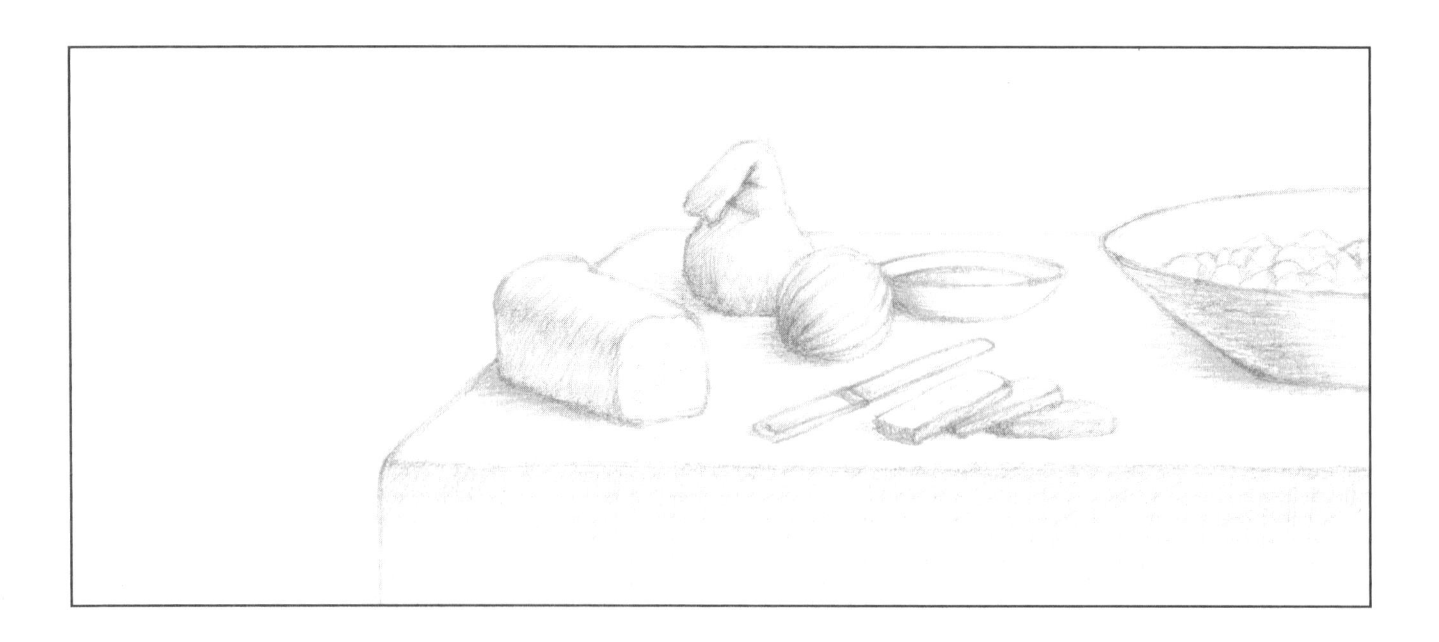

Old-Fashioned Bread Stuffing

- *8 slices white bread (toasted, cubed)*
- *1/2 teaspoon salt*
- *1 teaspoon pepper*
- *1/2 teaspoon paprika*
- *1 tablespoon poultry seasoning*
- *3/4 cup butter*
- *1 1/2 cups finely-chopped onion*
- *1 cup finely-chopped celery*
- *1 cup chicken broth*

Will stuff a 15 to 20-pound bird.

Combine toasted bread cubes, salt, pepper, paprika, and poultry seasoning in a large bowl. Melt butter in a large iron skillet over low heat. Add onion and celery. Cook 5 minutes, stirring often. Spoon onion, celery, and butter mixture over toast mixture. Then stir in chicken broth and mix well. Place in icebox until completely cooled. Stuff bird loosely. (Stuffing needs room to expand as it cooks.) Seal cavity with skewers, *or* sew closed with white thread. *Do not stuff bird until just before cooking.*

Your Notes:

Pecan Cranberry Relish

- *1 pound fresh cranberries*
- *2 navel oranges (peeled, cut into quarters)*
- *1 (16 oz.) jar crushed pineapple*
- *2 cups coarsely-chopped pecans*
- *1 cup diced celery*
- *1 cup superfine sugar*
- *1/4 teaspoon cayenne pepper*

Makes about 2 quarts.

Put cranberries in a colander. Discard any bad ones. Remove stems and rinse cranberries under cold running water. Use a meat grinder, with a medium-size blade, to grind cranberries and oranges into a large bowl. Strain pineapple and reserve the juice. Add crushed pineapple, pecans, celery, and sugar to bowl. Stir until well blended. Add 2 tablespoons of reserved pineapple juice and cayenne pepper. Stir to blend. Spoon mixture into 1-quart mason jars. Cover and let stand 1 to 2 hours. Then place in icebox. Tastes great with poultry or beef.

Grandfather would place an iron upside-down between his knees. Then he placed a pecan nut on the iron and used a hammer to crack open the nut.

Your Notes:

Relish with Fresh Vegetables

- 2 cups finely-diced red pepper
- 2 cups finely-diced green pepper
- 2 cups shredded cabbage
- 2 cups finely-chopped onion
- 1 cup finely-chopped red onion
- 4 tablespoons mustard seed
- 4 tablespoons salt
- 2 teaspoons celery seed
- 4 cups sugar
- 4 cups white vinegar
- 4 finely-chopped hot pepper pods

Makes about 4 quarts.

Day One: Combine all ingredients in a large bowl and mix well. Place in icebox overnight.

Day Two: Wash quart-size mason jars and lids in hot water. Then turn upside down to drain. When jars are cool, spoon in relish. Seal lids tightly and place in icebox. Serve chilled. Relish will keep for several weeks.

Your Notes:

Stuffing with Pecans

- *1/2 cup butter*
- *1 cup finely-chopped onion*
- *1/2 cup finely-chopped celery*
- *8 slices white bread (toasted, cubed)*
- *2 cups finely-chopped pecans*
- *1/2 cup chopped parsley*
- *2 teaspoons salt*
- *1/2 teaspoon pepper*
- *1 teaspoon poultry seasoning*
- *1/2 teaspoon sage*
- *1 cup chicken broth*

Will stuff a 12 to 15-pound bird.

In a large iron skillet, melt butter over low heat. Cook onion and celery 5 minutes. Put toasted bread cubes in a large bowl. Then spoon in onion, celery, and melted butter. Add pecans, parsley, salt, pepper, poultry seasoning, sage, and chicken broth. Mix well. Place in icebox until completely cooled. Stuff bird loosely. (Stuffing needs room to expand as it cooks.) Seal cavity with skewers, *or* sew closed with white thread. *Do not stuff bird until just before cooking.*

Your Notes:

Turkey Giblet Gravy

	giblets (neck, heart, gizzard and liver)	*1*	*teaspoon salt*
1	*celery stalk*		*turkey drippings*
1	*medium-size onion (peeled, cut in half)*	*1/3*	*cup flour*
2	*cups cold water*		

Makes about 1 1/2 cups.

While turkey is cooking: Rinse giblets and celery under cold running water. Cut celery into 1-inch pieces. Put celery and giblets in a 2-quart saucepot. Add onion, water, and salt. Cover and simmer over low heat 45 minutes. Using a slotted spoon, remove giblets from liquid and place in a bowl to cool. Remove and discard onion and celery. Reserve the liquid. Dice giblets. Remove meat from neck and chop finely.

When turkey is done: Place on a warm serving platter. Pour all drippings from roasting pan into a large glass measuring cup. Allow to stand until fat floats to the top. Return 5 tablespoons of fat to roasting pan. Remove and discard remaining fat from measuring cup. Return drippings to pan. Place roasting pan on top of stove over low heat. Using a spoon, stir and scrape sides and bottom of pan to loosen browned drippings. To prevent lumping, sprinkle flour slowly into roasting pan while stirring with a fork until mixture is smooth. Slowly stir in reserved liquid from giblets. Simmer 5 minutes, stirring frequently, until thickened. Stir giblets and neck meat into gravy and pour into a serving bowl.

Your Notes:

Desserts

When Grandmother made pies, she would begin early in the morning. First she made the dough, rolled it out, and placed it in pie pans. Then she prepared all of the ingredients for the fillings. She would mix them together, sometimes adding Grandfather's corn likker, and pour the mix into the pie crusts. Soon after she placed the pies in the oven, the whole house smelled of sweet potato and spice or something else nice.

Apple Pie

2 9-inch pie crusts (See my recipe, page 152.)
6 tart green apples (Granny Smith apples)
4 tablespoons fresh lemon juice
1 1/4 cups sugar
4 tablespoons all-purpose flour
1 1/2 teaspoons ground cinnamon
1/2 teaspoon ground nutmeg
4 tablespoons butter

Serves 6 to 8.

Prepare pie crusts. Place bottom crust in pie pan and set aside. Preheat oven to 375° F. Peel and core apples. Remove any remaining seeds. Slice into thin pieces and put into a large bowl. Add lemon juice and stir, making sure that all slices are well coated. *This keeps apples from turning brown.* Combine sugar, flour, cinnamon, and nutmeg in another bowl. Stir to blend. Add to apples and mix well. Spoon apples into bottom crust. Dot with butter. Cover with top crust. Fold edge of top crust under edge of bottom crust. Using a fork, press edges of both crusts together to seal pie. Make 4 slits in center of crust. *This allows steam to be released.* Bake 45 to 60 minutes, until crust is golden brown and juices are bubbling. (If crust begins to brown too quickly, cover with dampened brown paper. Remove brown paper the last 5 minutes of baking.) Remove from oven and let cool for about 30 minutes. Delicious hot or cold.

Your Notes:

Apricot Brandy Pound Cake

- *1 cup butter*
- *3 cups sugar*
- *6 eggs*
- *3 cups sifted all-purpose flour*
- *1/4 teaspoon baking soda*
- *1/2 teaspoon salt*
- *1 cup buttermilk*
- *1 teaspoon rum*
- *1 teaspoon orange extract*
- *1/4 teaspoon almond extract*
- *1/2 teaspoon lemon juice*
- *1 teaspoon vanilla*
- *1/2 cup apricot brandy*

Serves 12.

About 30 minutes before starting recipe, set out butter, buttermilk, and eggs. These should be room temperature before beginning.

Preheat oven to 325° F. Generously grease a 10-inch tube pan with lard. Lightly flour pan and set aside. In a large bowl, cream butter with a wooden spoon. Gradually add sugar, beating until light and fluffy. Add eggs, one at a time, and beat well after each egg is added. Into a second bowl, sift flour, baking soda, and salt together. In a third bowl, combine buttermilk, rum, extracts, lemon juice, vanilla, and brandy. Mix thoroughly. Alternately and gradually add flour mixture and buttermilk mixture to sugar mixture, beating after each addition. Pour batter into tube pan. Bake approximately 1 hour 10 minutes, *or* until a toothpick inserted into center comes out clean. Remove from oven. Wait 10 minutes. Then remove from pan. Let cool on cake rack.

Straws from a broom were washed and stored in a jar on the kitchen counter or in the cupboard. They were used to test cakes and breads for doneness.

Your Notes:

Apricot Peach Cobbler

Lattice-Top Pie Crust (See my recipe, page 145.)
- 1 *(16 oz.) jar peeled apricots*
- 6 *fresh large peaches*
- 4 *tablespoons fresh lemon juice*
- 6 *tablespoons butter*
- 2 *tablespoons all-purpose flour*
- 1 *cup sugar*
- 3/4 *teaspoon ground nutmeg*
- 1/4 *teaspoon salt*

Serves 12.

Generously grease a 9x13x2-inch baking pan with lard and set aside. Prepare pie crusts. Place bottom crust in baking pan and set aside. Preheat oven to 375° F. Drain apricots, reserving 1 cup of the juice. Peel peaches, cut in half, remove pits, and slice. Combine apricots and peaches in a large bowl. Add lemon juice and stir, making sure that all slices are well coated. *This keeps the peaches from turning brown.* Set peaches aside. Over low heat melt butter in a 2-quart saucepan. Using a wooden spoon, slowly stir in flour until smooth. Add sugar, nutmeg, and salt. Gradually stir in apricot and peach juices. Continue cooking, stirring until mixture thickens. Pour mixture over peaches and apricots. Stir to blend. Pour peach mixture into bottom crust and cover with lattice strips. Bake 35 to 45 minutes, *or* until crust is golden brown and juices are bubbling. Remove from oven and allow to cool at least 30 minutes.

Your Notes:

Blackberries

Picking blackberries was a fun chore, but we had to be very careful because the blackberry thickets had many black snakes. There were about six of us kids. We would spread out trying to see who could fill their pails first; whoever did, would be rewarded with a large lollipop. When our pails were full, we rushed home so Grandmother could make blackberries and dumplings.

Blackberries'n Dumplings

2 quarts fresh blackberries
6 cups cold water
1 1/2 cups sugar
1/2 teaspoon ground nutmeg
1 teaspoon vanilla
1/4 teaspoon salt

Serves 6 to 8.

Put blackberries in a colander. Gently rinse under cold running water. Put water in a large saucepot. Add sugar and blackberries. Bring to a boil. Then lower heat. Cover and simmer 15 minutes. Then stir nutmeg, vanilla, and salt into blackberries. Cover and simmer 15 minutes more.

After adding vanilla, nutmeg, and salt to blackberries begin making dumplings.

Dumplings:

2 cups sifted all-purpose flour
1 teaspoon salt
3 teaspoons baking powder
3 tablespoons sugar
2 tablespoons butter
3/4 cup milk

In a sifter, combine flour, salt, baking powder, and sugar. Sift into a medium-size bowl. Stir to mix. Melt butter and add to milk. Gradually add milk mixture to bowl of dry ingredients while stirring with a fork. Continue stirring until well blended and dough is smooth. Immediately scoop rounded tablespoons from dough and drop directly into blackberry sauce. Cover. Cook 15 minutes before removing lid. Then turn dumplings gently with fork. Cover and cook 10 minutes more. Serve hot with lots of homemade whipped cream. *(See my recipe, page 157.)*

Blackberry sauce is great over homemade ice cream. *(See my recipes, page 144.)*

Bourbon Sweet Potato Pie

1 9-inch pie crust (See my recipe, page 152.)
2 pounds sweet potatoes
1/2 cup butter
1/2 teaspoon ground cinnamon
1/8 teaspoon ground cloves
1/8 teaspoon ground ginger
1/4 teaspoon salt
1/2 cup firmly-packed light brown sugar
1/2 cup sugar
3 eggs
3/4 cup light cream
1/4 cup bourbon

Serves 8 to 10.

About 30 minutes before starting recipe, set out butter, cream, and eggs. These should be room temperature before beginning.

Prepare pie crust. Place in pie pan and set aside. Using a vegetable brush, scrub sweet potatoes under cold running water. Cut off any stems. Put sweet potatoes in a large pot and cover with cold water. Bring to a boil. Lower heat and cook until tender, approximately 30 minutes. Drain sweet potatoes and let cool. Peel sweet potatoes, put into a large bowl and mash until smooth. Add butter, cinnamon, cloves, ginger, and salt. Mix until butter melts. Add both sugars, eggs, cream, and bourbon. Using an egg beater, beat until blended. Preheat oven to 350° F. Place a sieve over another large bowl and press mixture through sieve. *This will remove any strings or lumps.* Pour mixture into pie crust. Bake 45 to 50 minutes, *or* until firm. Remove from oven. Cool 1 hour until set.

Your Notes:

Butter Drop Cookies

1 cup butter
2/3 cup sugar
2 eggs
1 teaspoon vanilla
1 1/2 cups twice-sifted all-purpose flour

Makes 4 dozen.

About 30 minutes before starting recipe, set out butter and eggs. These should be room temperature before beginning.

Preheat oven to 400° F. Generously grease a cookie sheet with lard. Using a wooden spoon, cream butter in a large bowl. Gradually add sugar, while beating, until light and fluffy. Add eggs and vanilla. Beat to blend. Slowly fold in flour to create dough. Scoop rounded teaspoonfuls of dough from bowl. Using a second spoon, push dough onto cookie sheet, 2 inches apart. Bake 10 minutes, *or only until edges of cookies are golden brown.* Remove from oven. Use a spatula to place cookies on a wire rack, and allow them to cool. *Handle with care. These cookies are very fragile.*

Baking cookies is a great experience for children.

Your Notes:

Clara's Bread Pudding

4 cups milk
3/4 cup sugar
6 teaspoons butter
1 1/2 teaspoons ground cinnamon
1/2 teaspoon ground nutmeg
6 cups cubed toast
4 eggs (lightly beaten)
3/4 cup seedless raisins

Serves 6 to 8.

About 30 minutes before starting recipe, set out butter, milk, and eggs. These should be room temperature before beginning.

Preheat oven to 325° F. Generously butter a 2-quart casserole dish. Combine milk, sugar, and butter in a medium-size saucepot. Heat until hot. Do not boil. Remove from heat and stir in cinnamon and nutmeg. Put toast in a large bowl. Pour mixture in and stir. Add eggs and raisins. Stir to blend. Pour mixture into casserole dish. Bake 45 to 60 minutes, *or* until a knife inserted into center comes out clean. Serve warm with a little light cream over each portion.

Your Notes:

Coconut Layer Cake

- 1 *fresh brown coconut*
- 1 *cup coconut milk*
- 2 *cups sugar*
- 3/4 *cup butter*
- 3 *eggs (separated)*
- 2 *cups whole milk*
- 1 1/2 *teaspoons vanilla*
- 3 *cups twice-sifted all-purpose flour*
- 3 *teaspoons baking powder*
- *fluffy white frosting (See my recipe, page 139)*

Makes one 4-layer cake.

About 30 minutes before starting recipe, set out butter, whole milk, and eggs. These should be room temperature before beginning. Separate eggs while they are cold. Crack each egg and separate whites into one small bowl and yolks into a second bowl.

Drive a nail through the eyes of the coconut. Drain coconut milk into a 1 cup measure and add enough whole milk to fill the 1 cup measure. Set aside. Then crack shell and remove meat. Peel off brown skin and discard. Grate coconut. Set aside for frosting. Preheat oven to 350º F. Generously grease the bottoms and sides of four (9-inch) cake pans with lard. Line bottom of pans with brown paper and grease with lard. Then lightly dust the sides and bottoms with flour. In a large bowl, cream sugar and butter until light and fluffy. Add egg yolks and beat well. Add coconut milk, whole milk, and vanilla to butter mixture. Stir well with a wooden spoon. In a large sifter, combine flour and baking powder. Then sift into butter mixture, a little at a time, beating well after each addition. Beat egg whites until soft peaks form. Then fold egg whites into batter until batter is smooth. Pour batter into cake pans. Bake 25 to 30 minutes, *or* until a toothpick inserted into center comes out clean. Cool 10 minutes in pans. Then remove from pans and put on cake racks. *If cake is left in pan longer than 10 minutes, it may be difficult to remove.* Cool thoroughly. Then peel off brown paper. If layers are uneven, use a large sharp knife to slice off uneven parts.

Frosting a cake: Use approximately 1/4 of frosting and coconut on top and sides of each layer. Use hand to spread coconut on sides. Put a dab of frosting on the center of a cake plate. *This keeps the cake from moving.* Position first layer, top side down, on plate. Cover with frosting and coconut. Position second layer, top side up. Cover with frosting and coconut. Position third layer, top side down. Cover with frosting and coconut. Position fourth layer, top side up. Cover with frosting and coconut.

Coconut Pecan Treats

1 fresh brown coconut
1 cup twice-sifted all-purpose flour
1 tablespoon brown sugar
1/2 cup butter
2 eggs
1/2 teaspoon vanilla
1/2 cup coarsely-chopped pecans
1 1/2 cups firmly-packed light brown sugar
1/2 teaspoon baking powder

Makes 16 squares.

About 30 minutes before starting recipe, set out butter and eggs. These should be room temperature before beginning.

Drive a nail through the eyes of the coconut. Drain coconut milk. Then crack shell and remove meat. Peel off brown skin and grate. Preheat oven to 350º F. Generously grease an 8x8x2-inch baking pan with lard. In a small bowl, mix flour, brown sugar, and butter until mixture resembles coarse cornmeal. Press mixture into pan to cover bottom. Bake 15 minutes. While crust is baking, combine eggs, vanilla, pecans, light brown sugar, 1 cup coconut, and baking powder in a large bowl. Beat well to blend. Remove pan from oven. Spoon mixture over crust to cover it completely. Return pan to oven and bake 30 minutes more. Remove from oven and cool in pan. While still warm, cut into squares.

Great recipe to do with children!

Your Notes:

Confectioners' Sugar Pound Cake

- *1 pound butter*
- *1 pound sifted confectioners' sugar*
- *6 eggs (lightly beaten)*
- *3 cups cake flour*
- *1 teaspoon vanilla*
- *1/2 teaspoon almond extract*
- *1/2 teaspoon lemon juice*
- *1 teaspoon rum*

Serves 10 to 12.

About 30 minutes before starting recipe, set out butter and eggs. These should be room temperature before beginning.

Preheat oven to 325° F. Generously butter bottom and sides of a 10-inch tube pan. Line bottom of pan with brown paper and grease with butter. Dust bottom and sides lightly with flour. Using a wooden spoon, cream butter in a large bowl. Gradually add confectioners' sugar, while beating, until light and fluffy. Add eggs and beat until blended. Gradually add flour to bowl while beating. Add vanilla, almond extract, lemon juice, and rum. Blend well. Then pour batter into pan. Bake 1 hour, *or* until a toothpick inserted into center comes out clean. Remove from oven and let stand 10 minutes. Then remove from pan. Put on a cake rack to cool. *If cake is left in pan longer than 10 minutes, it may be difficult to remove.* When cake is cooled, place on a cake plate and sprinkle with confectioners' sugar.

Confectioners' sugar, or powdered sugar, was also known as XXXX sugar.

Your Notes:

Fresh Baked Peach Halves

- *4 fresh large peaches*
- *2 tablespoons fresh lemon juice*
- *2 cups crushed corn flakes*
- *1/2 cup melted butter*
- *1/2 cup firmly-packed brown sugar*

Serves 8.

Preheat oven to 400° F. Generously grease a 9x13x2-inch baking pan with butter. Rinse peaches under cold running water. Cut into halves and remove pits. Put in a large bowl. Sprinkle with lemon juice and stir, making sure each half is well coated. *This keeps peaches from turning brown.* Then coat with corn flakes. Place cut side down in pan. Pour melted butter over peaches. Then sprinkle with brown sugar. Bake 30 minutes, *or* until lightly browned. Serve a hot peach with homemade ice cream or whipped cream. *(See my recipes.)*

This is a fun dish that children can help make!

Your Notes:

Frostings

Fluffy White Frosting:

- *3 cups sugar*
- *1/2 cup water*
- *2 egg whites (room temperature)*
- *1 teaspoon vanilla*

Frosts one four-layer cake.

Combine sugar and water in a medium-size saucepot. Bring to a rapid boil. Stir until all sugar *(including any around the sides of the pot)* is completely dissolved. *This will prevent frosting from becoming grainy in texture.* Continue to cook until mixture has the consistency of syrup, about 3 minutes. Turn heat off. Using an eggbeater, beat egg whites until soft peaks form. Continue beating and slowly add the syrup while still hot. *The hot syrup cooks the egg whites and the continuous beating adds air to frosting making it fluffy.* Then add vanilla and beat until well blended and frosting is thick enough to spread. *Use immediately.*

Cakes should be completely cooled before frosting. Frosting helps to keep the cake fresh and moist. Frosted cakes should be stored in the icebox.

Chocolate Frosting:

- *3/4 cup butter*
- *2 cups sugar*
- *1/2 cup cocoa*
- *1/2 cup milk*
- *1 teaspoon vanilla*

Frosts one 3-layer cake.

To prevent sugar crystals from forming when mixture bubbles, coat sides of saucepan with butter. Then melt butter over low heat in a medium-size saucepan. Add sugar, cocoa, and milk. Cook, stirring constantly, until sugar dissolves, approximately 2 minutes. Pour mixture into a small bowl. Place in icebox until completely cooled. Then add vanilla and beat with an eggbeater, until well blended and frosting is thick enough to spread. *Use immediately.*

Georgia Coffee Pound Cake

1/2	*cup strong perked coffee*	4	*eggs (lightly beaten)*
1/4	*cup milk*	2	*cups cake flour*
1	*cup butter*	2 1/2	*teaspoons baking powder*
1	*cup sugar*	1/4	*teaspoon mace*

Serves 10 to 12.

About 30 minutes before starting recipe, set out butter, milk and eggs. These should be room temperature before beginning.

Preheat oven to 325° F. Generously butter the bottom and sides of a 10-inch tube pan. Line bottom of pan with brown paper and grease paper with butter. Then lightly dust the sides and bottom with flour. Combine coffee with milk and set aside. In a large bowl, cream butter with a wooden spoon. Add sugar and beat until smooth and creamy. Add eggs and beat well. Combine flour, baking powder, and mace. Slowly add to butter mixture. While beating, add coffee mixture and beat until batter is smooth. Pour batter into pan. Bake 1 hour 15 minutes, *or* until a toothpick inserted into center comes out clean. Let cool in pan 10 minutes. Then remove from pan and place on cake rack. *If cake is left in pan longer than 10 minutes, it may be difficult to remove.* Allow to cool completely on rack before adding topping.

Topping:

1	*tablespoon hot strong perked coffee*	2	*teaspoons brandy*
2	*tablespoons sugar*	1/2	*pint chilled heavy cream*

Before starting recipe, chill a medium-size bowl and a whisk, or eggbeater.

Pour hot coffee into a cup and add sugar. Stir until sugar is dissolved. Stir in brandy and place in icebox to cool. Put heavy cream in chilled bowl and whip until it thickens and forms firm peaks. Then gently fold cooled coffee mixture into whipped cream. Spoon topping onto thinly sliced portions of pound cake.

Georgia Yam Pone

4 to 6 medium-size yams
1 cup butter (melted)
2 eggs (lightly beaten)
1/2 cup molasses
1 1/2 cups sugar
2 cups milk
1 cup all-purpose flour
1 teaspoon ground nutmeg
1 teaspoon ground cinnamon
1 teaspoon salt
2 teaspoons vanilla

Serves 10 to 12.

Preheat oven to 325° F. Generously grease a 3-quart casserole dish with butter. Grate yams to measure 4 cups. Combine yams, butter, eggs, molasses, sugar, and milk in a large bowl. Stir until well blended. Combine flour, nutmeg, cinnamon, and salt in a small bowl. Add flour mixture to yam mixture a little at a time to create a batter. Mix well after each addition. Stir in vanilla. Pour batter into casserole dish. Bake 2 hours 30 minutes. Stir several times during the first hour of baking. Serve hot.

Your Notes:

Glenauva's Chocolate Cake

1	*cup cocoa*
1	*cup boiling water*
1	*cup butter*
2 1/2	*cups sugar*
4	*eggs*
1 1/2	*teaspoons vanilla*
2 3/4	*cups sifted all-purpose flour*
2	*teaspoons baking soda*
1	*teaspoon baking powder*
1/2	*teaspoon salt*
	chocolate frosting
	(See my recipe, page 139.)

Makes one 3-layer cake.

About 30 minutes before starting recipe, set out butter and eggs. These should be room temperature before beginning.

Preheat oven to 350º F. Generously grease the bottoms and sides of three 9-inch cake pans with lard. Line bottom of pans with brown paper and grease with lard. Then lightly dust the sides and bottoms with flour. Combine cocoa and water in a small bowl. Stir well with a wooden spoon until smooth. Set aside to cool. Using a wooden spoon, cream butter and sugar in a large bowl until smooth. Add eggs, one at a time, beating well after each is added. Add vanilla and stir to blend. In a large sifter, combine flour, baking soda, baking powder, and salt. Sift into butter mixture, alternating with cooled cocoa. Stir well to blend. Pour batter into cake pans. Bake approximately 30 minutes, *or* until a toothpick inserted into the centers comes out clean. Let cool 10 minutes. Remove from pans and place on cake racks. *If cake is left in pan longer than 10 minutes, it may be difficult to remove.* Let cool completely. Then peel off brown paper. If layers are uneven, use a large sharp knife to slice off uneven parts.

Frosting a cake: Use approximately 1/3 of frosting on top and sides of each layer. Put a dab of frosting on the center of a cake plate. *This keeps the cake from moving.* Position first layer, top side up, on plate and frost. Position second layer, top side down, and frost. Position third layer, top side up, and frost.

Holiday Chews

- *2 eggs*
- *1 cup sugar*
- *1 teaspoon vanilla*
- *1 teaspoon orange extract*
- *1 teaspoon almond extract*
- *1/4 cup all-purpose flour*
- *1/4 teaspoon salt*
- *1 teaspoon baking powder*
- *1 cup chopped pecans*
- *1 cup chopped dates*
- *1 cup confectioners' sugar*

Makes 16 squares.

Preheat oven to 350º F. Generously grease an 8x8x2-inch pan with lard. In a medium-size bowl, beat eggs until light and fluffy. Add sugar, vanilla, orange extract, and almond extract. Beat until well blended. Combine flour, salt and baking powder in a sifter. Sift into egg mixture. Beat well to create a smooth batter. Lightly coat pecans and dates with flour and stir into batter. Pour batter into baking pan. Bake 30 minutes. Remove from oven. Cut into squares while warm. Remove from pan. Dust each square with confectioners' sugar and serve.

I remember looking forward to the sugarcane harvest. The men would cut the sugarcane in half, then push the pieces into a barrel with a turning blade inside. I watched as horses went around and around turning the millstone that ground the cane. The sugar dropped to the bottom, and the liquid floated up making a syrup. Grandfather would divide this among the neighbors who had come to help. My brother, the neighbors' kids and I would dip our cups into the liquid to taste the sweetness. Oh, so good! For us that was better than candy.

Homemade Ice Cream

This recipe is for the old-fashioned, hand-cranked ice cream maker.

2/3 cup sugar
2 cups cold milk
1 tablespoon vanilla
1/4 teaspoon salt
2 cups cold heavy cream

8 cups chopped ice and 1 cup coarse rock salt are required to freeze ice cream in a 2-quart container

Makes 1 1/2 quarts.

Vanilla Ice Cream: Pour sugar into saucepot and add 1/2 cup milk. Stir over a very low flame until sugar dissolves. Pour into a large bowl and place in icebox until thoroughly cooled. Remove bowl from icebox. Then add vanilla, salt, cream, and remaining milk. Stir to blend. Once the dasher (beater) and container are in place, pour chilled ice cream mixture into container to 2/3 full. Put the lid on and put the crank in place. The crank should turn freely. When the crank is turned clockwise, the dasher and container will turn. Alternate layers of ice and rock salt around the container. Turn crank after each layer is added to prevent packing it too tightly -- otherwise container will not move freely. Continue to fill well to the top. For the first 3 minutes, turn crank slowly. Then turn rapidly. *Cranking should be continuous for best results.* When cranking becomes difficult, the ice cream is ready. When ice cream is frozen, remove ice and rock salt to about 1 inch below the top. Wipe rock salt off top of lid. Then remove lid, take out the dasher and scrape clean. Serve at once, *or* replace lid and drain water. Then re-pack with ice and rock salt. *Best if allowed to set 2 hours so flavors can peak.*

For ice cream with fruit: Follow directions above, replacing vanilla with choice of fruit. Prepare fruit as follows:
Peach Ice Cream: Peel and slice 4 large peaches. Remove and discard pits. Mash with a potato masher.
Strawberry Ice Cream: Hull, slice and mash 1 pint fresh strawberries.
Banana Ice Cream: Peel, slice and mash 4 medium-size bananas.

Great recipe to do with children.

Lattice-Top Pie Crust

5 cups all-purpose flour
4 teaspoons salt
1 cup lard
1 cup ice water

Makes two pie crusts for a 9x13x2-inch baking pan.

Sift flour and salt together into a large bowl. Add lard. Cut lard into flour with a fork until mixture resembles coarse cornmeal. Add water, one tablespoon at a time, while mixing with fork until a moist dough is formed. Lightly flour hands and form dough into two balls.

Preparing Bottom Crust: Place one portion of dough on a lightly floured surface. Using a lightly floured rolling pin, roll out dough to make a rectangle 3 inches larger than pan on all sides. Fold dough in half and in half again. Place folded dough into baking pan and carefully unfold. Press dough against bottom and sides of pan. Trim excess, leaving 1/2 inch to hang over sides.

Preparing Lattice-Top Crust: Roll out second portion of dough to make a 12x13-inch rectangle. Cut 12 strips, 13 inches long by 1/2 inch wide. Place strips lengthwise on top of filling 1/4 inch apart. Re-roll remaining dough to form a 9x13-inch rectangle. Cut 18 strips, 9 inches long by 1/2 inch wide. To form a lattice pattern, weave strips directly on pie. *(Fold back alternating lengthwise strips. Place first short strip crosswise over long strips. Return folded strips to original position. Continue pattern by placing short strips 1/4 inch apart over alternating long strips to complete top crust.)* With fingertip, lightly moisten edges of bottom crust with water. Fold overhanging edges of bottom crust over edges of lattice strips. To seal edges, press dough with a fork that has been dipped in flour.

Your Notes:

Mama's Gingerbread

- *2 3/4 cups sifted all-purpose flour*
- *1/2 teaspoon baking soda*
- *3 teaspoons baking powder*
- *1 teaspoon ground cinnamon*
- *1/2 teaspoon ground cloves*
- *1 tablespoon ground ginger*
- *1 1/2 cups butter*
- *1 cup firmly-packed light brown sugar*
- *2 eggs (lightly beaten)*
- *3/4 cup molasses*
- *1 cup milk*

Makes 24 squares.

About 30 minutes before starting recipe, set out butter, milk, and eggs. These should be room temperature before beginning.

Preheat oven to 325° F. Generously grease the bottom and sides of a 9x13x2-inch cake pan with lard. Line bottom of pan with brown paper and grease with lard. Then lightly dust the sides and bottom with flour. Into a large bowl, sift flour, baking soda, baking powder, cinnamon, cloves, and ginger. Set aside. In another large bowl, cream butter with a wooden spoon. Gradually add sugar and beat until light and fluffy. Add eggs and molasses. Stir well. Alternately add flour mixture and milk. Beat well after each addition. Pour batter into cake pan. Bake 45 minutes, *or* until a toothpick inserted into center comes out clean. Cool 5 minutes in pan. Then remove from pan and put on a cake rack. Peel off brown paper. Put gingerbread back into the cake pan. Cut into 2-inch squares. Serve warm with whipped cream. *(See my recipe.)*

Your Notes:

Old-Fashioned Bread Pudding

- *2 cups milk*
- *6 tablespoons butter*
- *3/4 cup sugar*
- *2 eggs (lightly beaten)*
- *1/4 teaspoon salt*
- *1 teaspoon ground cinnamon*
- *1/2 cup seedless raisins*
- *4 cups bread cubes*

Serves 6 to 8.

Preheat oven to 350° F. Generously butter a 2-quart baking dish. Scald milk in a small saucepot. Add butter, stir until butter is melted, then set aside. In a large bowl, combine sugar, eggs, salt, cinnamon, and raisins. Mix until thoroughly blended. Stirring constantly, pour milk mixture slowly into egg mixture. Put bread cubes into baking dish. Pour mixture over bread cubes. Bake 45 minutes, *or* until a knife inserted 1 inch from the edge comes out clean. Delicious *warm or cold* with light cream, or cold with whipped cream.

For best results, use 2 or 3-day-old bread.

Your Notes:

Old-Fashioned Pecan Pound Cake

8 eggs (separated)
2 3/4 cups sugar
1 pound butter
6 tablespoons sugar
3 1/2 cups all-purpose flour
1 teaspoon baking powder
1/2 cup heavy cream
1 teaspoon vanilla
2 teaspoons rum
1 cup finely-chopped pecans

Serves 8 to 12.

About 30 minutes before starting recipe, set out butter, cream, and eggs. These should be room temperature before beginning. Separate eggs while they are cold. Crack each egg and separate whites into one small bowl and yolks into a second bowl.

Preheat oven to 325° F. Generously grease the bottom and sides of a 10-inch tube pan with lard. Line bottom of pan with brown paper and grease with lard. Then lightly dust the sides and bottom with flour. Using a wooden spoon, cream butter in a large bowl. Slowly add sugar, beating until light and fluffy. Add egg yolks and mix well. Sift flour and baking powder into butter mixture. Stir in cream, vanilla, and rum to form batter. In another large bowl, beat egg whites with an eggbeater until soft peaks form. Then slowly add 6 tablespoons of sugar. Continue beating until stiff peaks form. Fold egg whites into batter until smooth. Lightly coat nuts with flour and fold into batter. Pour batter into tube pan. Bake 1 1/2 hours, *or* until a toothpick inserted into center comes out clean. Remove from oven and let stand 10 minutes. Then remove from pan and place on a cake rack. *If cake is left in pan longer than 10 minutes, it may be difficult to remove.* Cool thoroughly. Then peel off brown paper. Place cake right side up on plate. Sprinkle with confectioners' sugar.

Your Notes:

Peach Cobbler

10 fresh medium-size peaches
4 tablespoons fresh lemon juice
1/2 teaspoon ground cinnamon
2 cups sugar
1/2 cup butter (melted)
3/4 cup all-purpose flour
2 teaspoons baking powder
1/4 teaspoon salt
3/4 cup milk

Serves 6.

Preheat oven to 325º F. Generously butter a 10x6x2-inch baking dish. Rinse peaches under cold running water and pat dry. Cut into halves and discard pits. Peel peaches and discard skins. Slice peaches and put into a large bowl. Sprinkle lemon juice over peaches, while stirring to make sure each slice is well coated with juice. *This keeps the peaches from turning brown.* Add cinnamon and 1 cup of sugar. Stir gently to coat. Spoon peaches into baking dish. Pour butter over peaches. In a medium-size bowl, combine remaining sugar, flour, baking powder, salt, and milk. Stir mixture until well blended. Spoon batter over peaches. Bake 50 minutes, *or* until golden brown and juices are bubbling. Let cool slightly before serving. Serve with ice cream or topped with whipped cream. *(See my recipes.)*

Peach cobbler is synonymous with peach-picking time in the South. Traditionally, fresh peaches would be cooked and stored in mason jars for use all year long.

Your Notes:

Pecan Pie

- *1 9-inch pie crust (See my recipe, page 152.)*
- *1 cup dark corn syrup*
- *1 cup firmly-packed light brown sugar*
- *1/4 teaspoon salt*
- *1/3 cup butter (melted)*
- *1 teaspoon vanilla*
- *3 eggs*
- *1 1/2 cups pecan halves*

Serves 6 to 8.

About 30 minutes before starting recipe, set out eggs. They should be room temperature before beginning. Prepare pie crust. Place in pie pan and set aside. Preheat oven to 350° F. In a large bowl combine corn syrup, brown sugar, salt, butter, vanilla, and eggs. Stir well until blended. Pour batter into pie crust. Arrange pecans in a pleasing pattern on top of batter. Bake 50 minutes, *or* until puffed and firm to the touch. Remove from oven and allow to cool at least 30 minutes. Enjoy with whipped cream, or ice cream. *(See my recipes.)*

Your Notes:

Pecan Pumpkin Pie

- 1 9-inch pie crust (See my recipe, page 152.)
- 3 eggs
- 1 cup sugar
- 1 teaspoon ground cinnamon
- 1/4 teaspoon ground cloves
- 1/4 teaspoon ground nutmeg
- 1 teaspoon vanilla
- 1/2 cup dark corn syrup
- 1/4 teaspoon salt
- 1 cup canned pumpkin
- 3/4 cup pecan halves

Serves 6 to 8.

About 30 minutes before starting recipe, set out eggs. They should be room temperature before beginning. Prepare pie crust. Place in pie pan and set aside. Preheat oven to 350º F. In a large bowl, combine eggs and sugar. Beat well. Add cinnamon, cloves, nutmeg, vanilla, corn syrup, salt, and pumpkin. Mix well. Lightly coat nuts with flour. Fold into batter. Pour batter into pie crust. Bake approximately 45 minutes, *or* until puffed and firm to the touch. Remove from oven and allow to cool at least 30 minutes.

Our neighborhood had an abundance of pecan and black hickory nut trees. When the nuts ripened and fell from the trees, the neighborhood kids would gather them and their parents would share the nuts among the families. Grandmother was so excited about getting the hickory nuts. Grandfather would crack them open, and Grandmother would chop and add them to the cake she was making that day.

Your Notes:

Pie Crust

1 1/4	*cups all-purpose flour*	*1/4*	*cup lard*
1	*teaspoon salt*	*4*	*tablespoons ice water*

Makes one 9-inch pie crust.

In a sifter, combine flour and salt. Sift into a large bowl. Add lard. Cut lard into flour with a fork until mixture resembles coarse cornmeal. Add water, one tablespoon at a time, while mixing with a fork until a moist dough is formed. Lightly flour hands and form dough into a ball. Place dough on a lightly floured surface.

Preparing Bottom Crust: Using a lightly floured rolling pin, roll out dough evenly to make a circle 2 inches wider than pie pan. Fold dough in half and in half again. Place folded dough in pie pan and carefully unfold. Press dough against bottom and sides of pan. Trim excess, leaving 1/2 inch to hang over edge. Fold dough under itself, all the way around, to form a raised edge. Using two fingers, *or* a fork, press edge down all the way around.

2 1/2	*cups all-purpose flour*	*1/2*	*cup lard*
2	*teaspoon salt*	*8*	*tablespoons ice water*

Makes two 9-inch pie crusts.

Follow above directions and form two balls of dough.

Preparing Bottom Crust: Follow above directions, except trim dough to edge of pie pan.

Preparing Top Crust: Using a lightly floured rolling pin, roll out dough evenly to make a circle 2 inches wider than pie pan. Fold dough in half and in half again. Carefully place dough over 1/4 section of pie filling. Unfold dough half-way. Then unfold to cover remainder of pie. Trim excess, leaving 1/2 inch to hang over edge. Fold dough under bottom crust, all the way around, forming a raised edge. Using two fingers, *or* a fork, press edges of dough together. Make several slits in the center. *This allows steam to escape.*

Raisin Rice Pudding

- *3/4 cup uncooked short-grain rice*
- *4 cups milk*
- *1 teaspoon salt*
- *3/4 cup sugar*
- *4 tablespoons melted butter*
- *1 teaspoon rum*
- *1/2 cup seedless raisins*

Serves 6 to 8.

Preheat oven to 300° F. Grease a 9x13x2-inch baking dish with butter. Put rice in baking dish. Combine milk, salt, sugar, butter, and rum in a large bowl. Stir until blended. Pour over rice and stir until well mixed. Bake 1 1/2 hours, stirring every 15 minutes with a fork. Carefully turn the top under and scrape down the edges. Remove from oven. Stir in raisins. Return to oven and bake 30 minutes longer, *or* until rice is tender and pudding is creamy and thick.

Rice Pudding Without Raisins: Prepare as above, using 1 teaspoon vanilla instead of rum. Omit raisins.

Your Notes:

Strawberry Shortcake

2 quarts strawberries
1/3 cup fresh lemon juice
1 cup sugar
2 cups all-purpose flour
1/2 teaspoon salt
2 tablespoons baking powder
2 tablespoons sugar
4 tablespoons lard
3/4 cup milk

Serves 8.

Using a colander, gently rinse strawberries under cold running water. Remove caps and cut strawberries in half. In a large bowl, combine lemon juice and 1 cup sugar. Stir until sugar is dissolved. Stir in strawberries and place in icebox. Preheat oven to 350º F. Generously grease two 8-inch cake pans with lard. Sift flour, salt, baking powder and 2 tablespoons sugar into another large bowl and mix. Add lard and mix with a fork until mixture resembles coarse meal. Then gradually add milk, while stirring with fork, until mixture becomes a soft dough. Divide dough in half. Lightly flour hands. Then press dough evenly into each pan to cover entire bottom. Bake 25 to 30 minutes, *or* until light brown. Remove shortcakes from pans and place on a cake rack to cool. Place one shortcake on a plate. Spoon 1/2 the strawberries and 1/2 the juice onto top of cake. Put the other shortcake on top of strawberries. Cover top with remaining strawberries and juice. Serve topped with whipped cream. *(See my recipe.)*

Your Notes:

Sweet Potato Pudding

- 4 *cups boiled, mashed sweet potatoes*
- 3/4 *cup sugar*
- 2 *eggs*
- 4 *tablespoons butter (melted)*
- 1/2 *cup coconut milk*
- 1 *lime rind (finely grated)*
- 1 *tablespoon lime juice*
- 2 *tablespoons rum*
- 1/4 *teaspoon salt*
- 1/2 *teaspoon baking powder*
- 1/4 *cup seedless raisins*
- 2 *teaspoons ground cinnamon*

Serves 8.

Preheat oven to 350° F. Grease an 8x8x2-inch baking dish with butter and set aside. Put sweet potatoes in a large bowl. Add sugar, eggs, butter, and coconut milk. Beat vigorously until smooth. Stir in lime rind, lime juice, and rum. Mix well. Add salt, baking powder, raisins, and cinnamon. Mix well and pour into baking dish. Bake 50 to 60 minutes. Serve hot.

Your Notes:

Tipsy Sweet Potato Pone

6 medium-size sweet potatoes
2 tablespoons all-purpose flour
1 1/4 cups sugar
3 eggs
1 teaspoon ground cinnamon
1/2 teaspoon ground allspice
1 teaspoon ground nutmeg
2 1/2 cups milk
1/2 cup bourbon
1 cup coarsely-chopped pecans
1 cup butter (melted)
1/4 teaspoon salt

Serves 12.

Preheat oven to 325° F. Generously butter a 10x12x2-inch baking pan. Wash sweet potatoes well under running cold water and peel. Finely grate sweet potatoes to measure 3 cups. In a large bowl, combine flour, sugar, eggs, cinnamon, allspice, nutmeg, milk, and bourbon. Beat thoroughly to blend. Add sweet potatoes, pecans, butter, and salt to mixture. Stir thoroughly to blend. Pour mixture into baking pan. Bake 2 hours. Serve hot.

We didn't use bourbon in those days. Grandmother used homemade corn likker.

Your Notes:

Whipped Cream

2 cups cold heavy cream
1/2 cup sugar
1 teaspoon vanilla

Makes 2 cups.

Chill a medium-size bowl and an eggbeater in icebox prior to beginning recipe. Pour heavy cream into bowl and beat until slightly thickened. Add sugar a little at a time, beating after each addition. Add vanilla. Beat until firm peaks form. *Whipped cream will not break down for several hours in the icebox.* Delicious as a topping on pies and fruits.

After Grandmother milked the cows, she would put the milk into 5-inch high, round tin pans. Grandfather had built a little house in a tree where Grandmother set the milk to cool. The cream would rise to the top. She would skim it off and put it into a bowl. I loved to lick the eggbeater after Grandmother made whipped cream.

Your Notes:

Beverages

On hot summer days, Grandmother would take bright yellow lemons and roll them on the kitchen table until they were soft. Then she cut them, squeezed the juice into a large jar of cold water, and added in sugar. Sometimes, when Grandfather went fishing, he would take along a jar of lemonade.

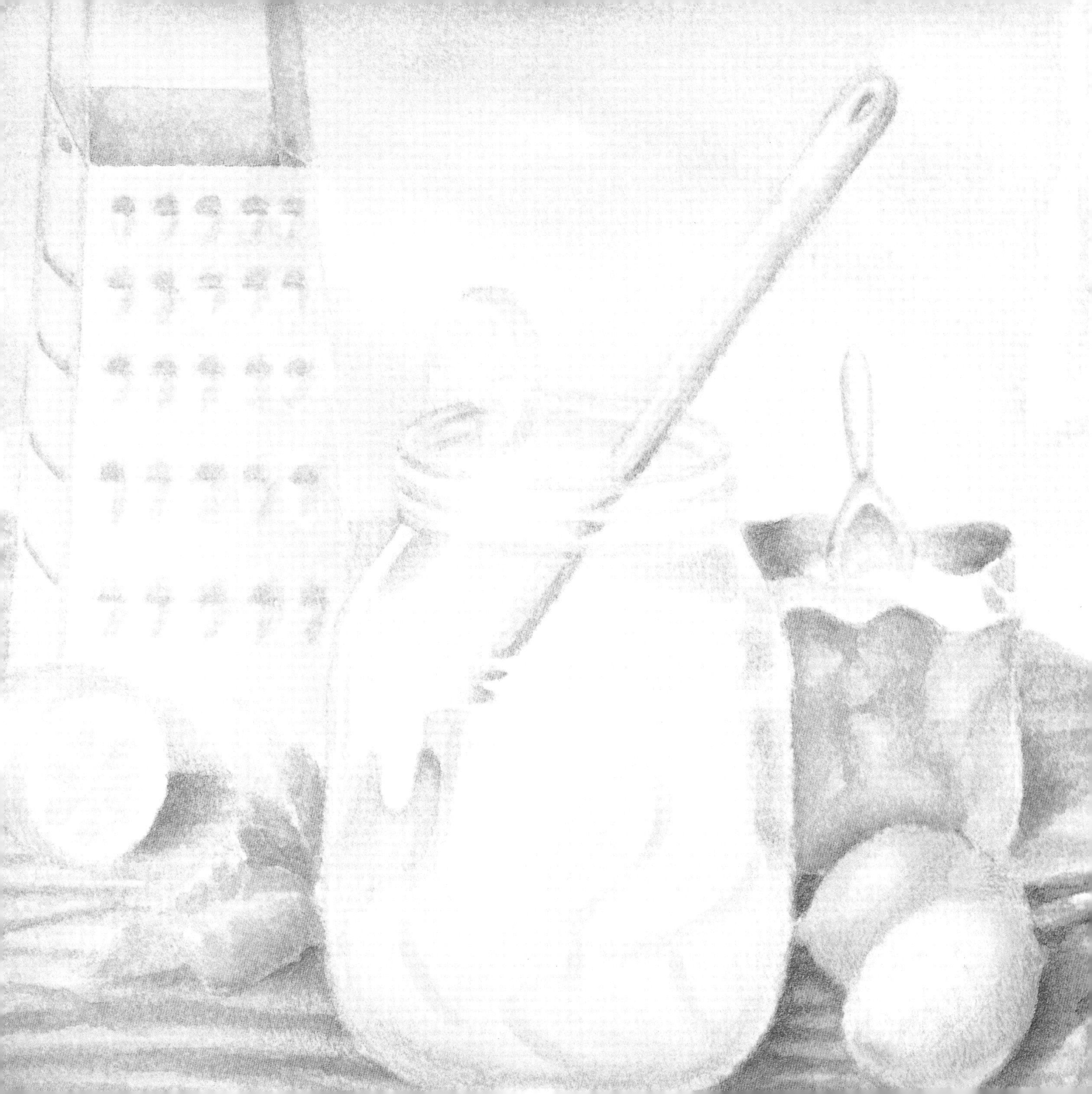

Beverages

Speckled-Pot Iced Tea

- *1 gallon cold water*
- *1/2 cup loose tea*

Makes 1 gallon.

Fill a large coffee pot with water. Fold a large piece of cheesecloth in half to make a square. Place tea in center of cheesecloth. Bring the corners together to form a pouch. Tie pouch with clean white string *or* white thread. Leave string long enough to tie around handle after placing pouch inside pot. Cover and set in sunlight. Let steep all day. Serve over ice with a wedge of lemon, or a sprig of mint.

The 8-quart speckled pots and the large speckled coffee pots were used for making beverages. These pots were always on the back burners of the stove. To make what we know today as sun tea, a pot of water with tea was usually set on the back porch to brew in the sunlight.

Old-Time Country Lemonade

- *1 1/2 cups cold water*
- *2 1/2 cups sugar*
- *12 medium-size lemons*
- *12 cups cold water*
- *4 lemons (thinly sliced)*

Makes 1 gallon.

Pour 1 1/2 cups of water into a large pot and bring to a boil. Add sugar and stir until sugar dissolves. Remove from heat and set aside to cool. Roll 12 lemons on tabletop until soft, and cut into halves. Squeeze juice into a small bowl. Remove seeds. *Do not strain out pulp.* Pour juice into sugar-water mixture. Add 12 cups cold water and stir well. Ladle into tall glasses filled with ice. Garnish with a slice of lemon. Pour remaining lemonade into a pitcher.

Lemonade was a summertime beverage usually made early in the morning. Grandmother would make enough to last the whole day. Grandfather liked to drink his from a jar.

Beverages

Hot Apple Cider

- 6 medium-size lemons
- 2 cups sugar
- 4 quarts apple cider
- 1/2 teaspoon ground nutmeg
- 1 teaspoon ground cloves
- 6 cinnamon sticks (broken in half)

Makes 4 quarts.

Roll lemons on tabletop until soft, then cut into halves. Squeeze juice into a small measuring cup. Strain juice into a large pot, and add sugar and cider. Bring to a boil. Remove from heat immediately. Put nutmeg and cloves in a small bowl. Pour 1/2 cup of hot cider over spices. Stir until blended. Add to pot and stir. Put a cinnamon stick into each cup of cider when served.

Buttermilk Drink

- 1 (8oz.) glass buttermilk
- 2 tablespoons corn syrup, or molasses

Serves 1.

Add syrup to a glass of buttermilk. Stir to blend. Serve with a square of Mama's gingerbread. *(See my recipe.)*

A lumpy, thicker buttermilk was known as clabber milk.

Your Notes:

Cooking Terms

Baste - Moisten food *(usually meat)* during cooking with melted butter, fat, pan drippings, glaze or sauce which add flavoring.

Beat - Add air to a mixture to make it smooth, using a consistent rapid motion that lifts the mixture up and over.

Blend - Combine ingredients thoroughly.

Chop - Cut into small irregular pieces.

Chutney - Thick sauce *(usually highly seasoned)* made of fruits and spices.

Coat - Cover evenly with chopped nuts, flour, sugar, or crumbs.

Confectioners' Sugar - Finely powdered sugar combined with cornstarch. *(Also known as XXXX.)*

Cool - Let stand at room temperature until no longer hot.

Cream - Soften a fat *(such as butter)* by beating until light and fluffy.

Crimp - Make crinkled or wavy *(as the edge of a pie crust).*

Cube - Cut into uniform pieces about 1/2 inch on all sides.

Cut in - Use a fork to work fat into flour.

Dash - 1/8 teaspoonful.

Deep-fat fry - Cook at high temperature in a deep pan with enough fat to cover food.

Dice - Cut into uniform pieces about 1/8 to 1/4 inch.

Dough - Mixture of flour or meal which is stiff enough to knead or roll.

Drippings - Fat or juices that settle to the bottom of the pan when cooking meats. *(Used for flavoring other foods such as collard greens and gravies).*

Dust - Lightly sprinkle food with flour or sugar.

Entrails - Intestines.

Fat back - Fatty strip from the back of a hog, usually cured by salting and drying.

Filé - Combination of powdered herbs and dried young sassafras leaves, used as a thickener and flavoring agent.

Fillet - (1) Piece of boneless meat or fish. (2) To cut into fillets.

Fold in - Combine one delicate ingredient *(such as beaten eggs or whipped cream)* with another ingredient *(such as a batter)* using a wooden spoon and a gentle under and over motion.

Grits - Coarsely ground hulled corn.

Gumbo - Thick soup usually made with okra or filé and a combination of other vegetables and seasonings.

Jambalaya - Rice cooked with meat, poultry or seafood, and seasoned with herbs.

Knead - To work dough with hands, folding over and pressing until smooth and elastic.

Lard - Fat made from hogs.

Pie crust - Dough formed to the shape of a pan used to cook pies. Also, dough used for top layer of pies.

Preheat - Heat oven to desired temperature before starting recipe.

Render - Extract fat by cooking.

Roe - Sack of fish eggs.

Roll out - Flatten *(as dough)* with a rolling pin.

Salt pork - Pork fat cured in salt.

Sift - Put dry ingredients through a sifter to remove lumps and add air.

Simmer - Cook just below the boiling point.

Slit - Make a shallow cut into a surface *(such as a fish belly, or a pie crust).*

Wedge - Tapered or v-shaped piece *(such as a lemon wedge).*

Whip - Beat rapidly to increase the volume of food by adding air.

XXXX - Confectioners' sugar.

Helpful Hints

Measuring Ingredients Accurately:

Dry ingredients: (Baking powder, baking soda, cinnamon, salt, etc.) Stir lightly with a fork or spoon to break up lumps before measuring. Then fill a spoon with a heaping amount and level off with a straight edge.

Granulated sugar: Measure with a measuring cup or spoon. *Do not tap or shake down.* Fill to the rim and then level off with a straight edge.

Brown sugar: Use a rolling pin to break up any lumps before measuring. Pack firmly in a measuring cup. *Air pockets can be eliminated by using the back of a spoon.* Then use a straight edge to level off.

Flour: Sift onto wax paper before measuring. Then gently pour into a measuring cup to rim. Level off with a straight edge. *Do not tap or shake down. That will undo the sifting process.*

Cornmeal: Stir lightly with a fork or spoon to break up lumps before measuring. *Do not sift.* Scoop into a measuring cup and level off with a straight edge.

Liquids: Use a standard measuring cup set on a level surface. Measured liquids should be read at eye level.

Oil and syrup: Measure the same as ***Liquids***. However, because oils and syrups cling, *scrape all* of the oil or syrup from measuring cup.

Shortening: Keep at room temperature for easy measuring. To eliminate air pockets pack into a measuring cup using the back of a spoon. Pack to the rim. Then level off using a straight edge.

Kneading Dough:

Work as quickly as you can. Place dough on a floured surface. Fold dough over on itself towards you. Then push dough down and away from you with the heels of both hands. Rotate dough 90° and repeat motions. Repeat this process until dough is smooth and elastic. *Soft dough makes tender and light biscuits and breads.*

Liquid Measures:

3 teaspoons (tsp.)	=	*1 tablespoon (tbsp.)*
4 tablespoons	=	*1/4 cup*
5 1/3 tablespoons	=	*1/3 cup*
8 tablespoons	=	*1/2 cup*
16 tablespoons	=	*1 cup*
1 cup	=	*8 fluid ounces (oz.)*
1 cup	=	*1/2 pint (pt.)*
2 cups	=	*1 pint*
4 cups	=	*1 quart (qt.)*
4 quarts	=	*1 gallon (gal.)*

Dairy Measures:

Cheese:

4 ounces	=	*1 cup shredded*
1 pound (lb.)	=	*4 cups shredded*

Butter:

1 stick	=	*1/2 cup*
4 sticks	=	*2 cups, or 1 pound*

Index

Index

MAKE A GIFT OF *Cookin' the Old-Time Southern Way with Venezuela*

ILLUSTRATED COOKBOOK WITH UNALTERED RECIPES, REFLECTIONS, AND HISTORICAL NOTES

To Order: **CALL:** (914)-244-0639 or **TOLL FREE:** 1-866-865-MENA(6362); Mon.- Fri., 9am-5pm, Eastern time

MAIL ORDERS TO: Mena Publishing, Inc., 487 East Main Street, #140, Mt. Kisco, New York, 10549

YES, I want______COPIES @ $19.95 EACH of: ***Cookin' the Old-Time Southern Way with Venezuela***

Shipping & Handling: **INCLUDE:** $4.95 FOR **ONE** BOOK, and $2.95 FOR EACH **ADDITIONAL** BOOK.

Payment: **MAKE CHECK** or **MONEY ORDER** PAYABLE TO: **Mena Publishing, Inc.**

CHARGE MY: ☐ **MASTERCARD** ☐ **VISA CARD** #____________________ **exp. date** ________

AMOUNT ENCLOSED $__________ ***(N.Y. State residents add 7.00% sales tax.)*** Allow 3 - 4 weeks for delivery.

(PLEASE PRINT)

NAME ____

ADDRESS ____

CITY ____________________ STATE __________ ZIP ________

TELEPHONE ________________ E-MAIL ____________________

PLEASE VISIT OUR WEB-SITE: www.menapublishinginc.com